MAKING SENSE

OF PRIMARY

INSPECTION

MAKING SENSE
OF PRIMARY
INSPECTION

Ian Sandbrook

Open University Press
Buckingham • Philadelphia

Open University Press
Celtic Court
22 Ballmoor
Buckingham
MK 18 1XW

and

1900 Frost Road, Suite 101
Bristol, PA 19007, USA

First Published 1996

A catalogue record of this book is available from the British Library

ISBN   0 335 19665 9 (hb)   0 335 19664 0 (pb)

Library of Congress Cataloging-in-Publication Data
Sandbrook, Ian, 1950–
     Making sense of primary inspection / Ian Sandbrook.
         p.   cm.
     Includes bibliographical references and index.
     ISBN 0-335-19665-9 (hardcover). — ISBN 0-335-19664-0 (pbk.)
     1. Elementary school administration—Great Britain.   2. Education, Elementary—
     Great Britain—Evaluation.   I. Title.
     LB2822.5.S36 1996
     379, 1´64—dc20   96–12681
                                                                                                            CIP

Typeset by Graphicraft Typesetters Ltd, Hong Kong
Printed and bound in Great Britain by
Biddles Ltd, Guildford and King's Lynn

CONTENTS

ACKNOWLEDGEMENTS

My thanks to all of the people who have helped me with this book and with the research project which preceded it. There are too many to name them all, but I owe a particular debt to those who agreed to be interviewed for my 12 case studies; to the Education Department of Hampshire County Council who funded my research project; to all of my colleagues, particularly Peter Newlands, Eric Gower and Margaret Simpson; to my supervisor at Sussex University, Tony Becher; and to Catherine, Rachel and William Sandbrook for their patient support.

INTRODUCTION

In September 1994, the Office for Standards in Education (Ofsted) began to inspect primary schools. Many schools have now been inspected under the Ofsted procedures and many others await their turn with some trepidation. This book explores what actually happens in an inspection and sets out to help people to make sense of the experience.

The book is based on a research project involving over 80 interviews in 12 case studies of inspections which took place in a variety of types of primary schools in seven different local authorities. Although most of the case work was carried out before September 1994, all of the main findings of the research still apply to Ofsted inspections. I have drawn on my more recent experience as an Ofsted Registered Inspector and of working with schools before and after Ofsted inspections to ensure that what is said is as up to date as revisions to the Ofsted framework will allow.

At the outset of the research, the arrangements for a systematic programme of inspection of all schools were still being discussed in Parliament. As a member of a local education authority (LEA) inspection service, I was sceptical of the benefits of inspection to the individual schools being inspected. As Winkley (1985) has pointed out, there is 'no evident relation between inspectorial visits and the excellence of schools' (p. 11). He also wrote that 'nobody has ever explored, and certainly not in any systematic way, either the limits or the alternatives to inspection' (p. 221).

It was this scepticism of inspection as a development tool and this absence of evidence either way which led me to ask: how does a full inspection affect the life of a primary school and, in particular, the quality of its teaching and learning?

However, as I set about considering how this question might be answered, I found that I was, to an extent, trapped in a view of inspection which equated it to a force being applied to a stationary object, with an expectation that the object would move a measurable distance. This view is pervasive. Many people, including, it would appear, a number of those directly involved in inspection, seem to want to use a mechanical model which sees things in terms of input-process-output. Such a view expects inspection to be scientific, measuring outcomes with a high degree of certainty, using tests of validity and reliability with a sense of virtual proof.

A closer look at the internal workings of inspection has shown them to be conditional, negotiated and subject to the changes of human nature. All parties to inspections, be they teachers, inspectors, governors, parents, local or national politicians, may confuse – perhaps confound – judgement with proof. So the notion of inspection having an impact, in any measurable mechanical sense, has proved to be wide of the mark. As Henkel (1991) has suggested, it is inappropriate to depict inspection as somehow driving the school. In so far as any institution can drive another, it is more likely that the school will drive itself. In reality, the effects of an inspection are likely to be more percolative and interactive. As a result they are unlikely to be simple to observe or to attribute.

Nevertheless, there is an ideology within the political arena which expects inspection to make an impact. Expectations do exist for inspection to be a mechanism for quality control, quality assurance and accountability. Whether these expectations are realised in practice is more debatable. Recent developments suggest that perhaps these impacts occur more indirectly than directly; the advent of the Framework for the Inspection of schools (Ofsted 1992) has arguably had more impact than the inspections themselves.

The tension between a view which interprets the idea of assessment in a calibrated, measurable way, and an alternative view which recognises that there are values, perceptions and interpretations which may make assessment more negotiated and conditional, remained present throughout my research. I have had to wrestle with it and so did the people I interviewed.

Early on I discovered that there was a whole dimension to inspection whose significance I had seriously underrated. I had not realised the extent to which every teacher and headteacher has some preoccupation with the judgemental verdict of inspection. My initial concern with whether inspection makes a difference to the quality of what goes on in a school needed a sharp adjustment. I had been thinking developmentally – looking for suggestions of subsequent improvement. If there are people who are looking for something quite different in inspection, then my prior assumptions about its effects were wrong. If one were to pose an evaluative question about the 'success' of an inspection, it emerges that one could be looking for two distinct things: an accurate and fair account of the school which would provide a validation of its strengths and a catalogue of its weaknesses; or, alternatively, an accurate and fair diagnosis of the school's potential for development leading to a real likelihood that such development would occur.

As it has turned out, this is not an either-or choice. There is a repeated oscillation between the judgemental and the developmental interpretation of inspection. This is a core theme throughout the book.

A second major theme is the emotional response to inspection. The fact that an inspection is intended as an institutional review, with clear protocols about not naming individual teachers in reports, does not prevent individuals from feeling personally exposed. There is a strong personal response from headteachers and teachers, generating an agenda for inspectors which is not always addressed particularly sensitively. In this context, some teachers see themselves almost as victims resisting attack and there are others who emerge from the process more wounded than bruised.

The technical aspects of inspection follow a notably consistent format, generating expectations of what will occur and what should occur based on custom and practice. Behind this custom and practice a kind of mythology has developed, looming as a shadow over inspections, suggesting a worst-case scenario from which teachers are relieved to escape. Within this custom and practice, there are also ritualistic elements offering protection from difficult interactions, particularly at the beginnings and ends of inspections.

The idea of there being a mythology of inspection and associated rituals usually surfaces rather negatively. However, it is important to recognise that myth also represents a means of making sense. The very nature of this book is bound up in this notion. I consistently make connections between the similar and different ways in which things happen and search for why these things occur. The inspectors are trying to do this with the schools they inspect, and the teachers and headteachers invest different meanings in what transpires. Myth is one way of explaining things we only partially understand; partial understanding and subsequent mismatches of perception seem to be a feature of inspections.

The intense personal accountability that surfaces means that several teachers and headteachers look for ways of defending themselves against criticism, whether real, implied or imagined. This attempt to displace the inspection findings places considerable pressure on the inspectors to carry out their work in watertight ways. In this context, the issue of credibility is often identified. A key factor in the inspectors' credibility seems to be their behaviour in the classroom and, to an extent, in face-to-face interviews with teachers. There are other technical issues which teachers look to exploit but, in general terms, the ability of inspectors to relate to children in the classroom seems to be the most telling factor.

There has been considerable comment in the educational press about the distortion which the event of inspection causes to the practice which is being observed. It has been suggested that teachers might lay on special lessons, that policy documents are specially written, and that the inspectors do not gain a reliable picture from the contrived performance laid on by the school. In my research project, the views on this issue varied widely, making any reliable generalisation impossible. However, there is a different kind of distortion, whereby the inspectors tailor their findings and issues to their perception of the school's readiness to hear what they might have to say. This implicit negotiation of the inspection's findings serves to underline the conditional nature of the process. Inspectors do not always seem to 'report as they find, without fear or favour', as Lawton (1988: 193) has suggested was the normal practice of Her Majesty's Inspectors.

It was my original intention to explore the outcomes of inspection over a longer period of time. One of my initial case studies indicated that this would be very difficult. The pace of change within the world of education has been such that the particular influence of an inspection cannot easily be disentangled from other catalysts for change, such as the progressive implementation of the National Curriculum, staff turnover, particular issues raised by parents or governors, the initiatives of advisers or in-service training or the advent of grant-maintained status.

As a result, I have been dependent on people's perceptions of the likelihood that the inspection would directly influence subsequent action. In the event, an absence of follow-up interviews has been less of an issue than it might have been. I have moved from my initial position, where I was looking for and expecting clear effects of inspection on subsequent practice. The school's learning processes do not seem to work in this way, any more than the child's does. An inspection may sow a seed which bears fruit some time hence. It will depend on the ground into which it is sown and the way in which that ground is fed. Moreover, the emergence of the judgemental agenda meant that I found myself looking at a different kind of outcome from the one I had previously expected. The validation of a school's perception of itself which could be provided by an inspection report may help to strengthen a developmental dynamic which already existed. It is very difficult to assess the extent to which the inspection might contribute to subsequent development. This problem is compounded by the efforts of inspectors to avoid surprises, through the careful 'leakage' of findings, so that teachers and headteachers are convinced that they already knew what the inspectors would find, even when that doesn't always appear to be strictly true.

Through the exchanges of perception that occur in inspection, the notion of professionalism is never far away. There seems to be a relationship between the professional maturity of teachers and their readiness to look at inspection from a more formative standpoint. The success of inspectors in communicating their findings about the schools they inspect depends, at least in part, on the match between their view of professionalism and the teacher's own professionalism. Whilst professional confidence and competence determine how people react to inspection, the inspections themselves serve to define what professional competence is. In a sense, one of the most significant outcomes of inspection is a negotiated consensus about professional expectations.

1 THE CHANGING CULTURE OF INSPECTION

This chapter outlines the history of inspection over the past 20 years or so, placing it in the context of shifts in the culture and ideology of the world of primary education.

The contemporary position

In September 1994, the Office for Standards in Education (Ofsted) set in motion the first inspections of primary schools under the auspices of the Education (Schools) Act 1992. This Act had established Ofsted and required that all schools should be inspected every four years in accordance with a standard framework (*Framework for the Inspection of Schools* 1992, revised 1993, 1994 and 1995). This framework offers a code of conduct for inspectors, detailed procedural guidance, requirements for the size of the inspection team in relation to the size of the school, a schedule which provides the evaluation criteria, and a set of criteria to govern the standards and quality of inspection itself. Inspectors have to 'demonstrate that their judgements are:

(i) secure
(ii) first-hand
(iii) reliable
(iv) valid

(v) comprehensive, and
(vi) corporate.'

Since the Act became law in 1992, Ofsted has had to organise the accreditation of sufficient inspectors to lead and participate in the inspection teams
required to carry out the enormous task of inspecting every school every four
years.

The drafting, passing and implementation of the 1992 Act, supplemented
by provisions in the 1993 Education Act to deal with schools which might
be deemed to fall short of the expectations of the Ofsted inspectors, are the
latest episodes in the history of inspection. However, the strands of intention and ideology which have now been formally enshrined in a statutory
framework can be identified backwards in time. The dynamics and effects of
inspections which took place before the Ofsted framework have much more
in common with more recent inspections than they have differences.

Local authority inspection 1976–88

The genesis of the 1992 Education Act could be dated back to the establishment of an official inspectorate during the nineteenth century. It would not
be appropriate to rehearse the evolution of inspection over 120 years. We can
uncover inspection's salient ideological features if we start in 1976. In that
year the Prime Minister of the day, Jim Callaghan, made a speech at Ruskin
College, Oxford, where he called into question the 'secret garden' of education and the curriculum. It was in the same year that a primary school in
Islington, London, called William Tyndale Junior School, came to the attention of the press and public because of a conflict about curriculum between
different members of the school's staff. Both of these events suggested that
schools and their teachers needed to be more accountable to the public at
large.

In his report on the William Tyndale affair (1976: 16), Robin Auld, QC, explained that 'in keeping with the education authority's view that its Inspectorate's role is predominantly an advisory one, it does not provide for regular
full inspections of its schools. The Authority's policy is that full inspections
only take place where there is some "special reason".'

This is essentially the position that was still being taken in 1991 by the
authority in which I undertook the first two case studies of my research. Both
of these schools were being inspected because there was a special reason. In
one there was a concern about the school's attitudes to statutory assessment;
in the other, a concern about the quality of the school's management.

Following the Ruskin speech and the William Tyndale affair, there were
developments which began to tighten schools' accountability. The Inner
London Education Authority (ILEA) (1977) and several other local education
authorities developed checklists to support school self-evaluation, and the
ILEA did begin a systematic programme of full inspection, albeit at the rate
of about 20 primary schools per year. At that time, the prevailing view
was that schools were best placed to manage their own evaluation. This was

because evaluation was seen in terms of development and needed the ownership of the professionals who would have to implement any findings.

Nevertheless, Becher Eraut and Knight (1981), despite some advocacy of school self-evaluation, did give inspection full consideration in their exploration of educational accountability. They suggested that inspection was commonly accepted by the public, was seen by teachers as offering natural justice, was more humane than testing, was considered supportive by headteachers, and was more flexible than testing in taking account of extenuating circumstances. They also suggested that it could be superficial and impressionistic, professionally biased and prejudiced, and that a head or teacher could mislead the inspectors.

Auld, Becher and Eraut were looking at accountability in the context of the local education authorities (LEAs) who carried the responsibility for educational provision under the terms of the 1944 Education Act. The accountability function of the LEAs was carried out by their advisory services. The role of these services was spelt out in 1985 in a draft statement by the Secretary of State for Education and Science as:

1 monitoring and evaluating the work of the authority's services;
2 supporting schools and other educational establishments;
3 supporting and developing teachers and advising on their management;
4 working on local initiatives.

There were two significant problems: the size of these advisory services was small, despite a substantial increase in personnel during the early 1980s; and there was a consistent prioritisation of their support-development functions over their monitoring function. Winkley (1985), exploring the work of advisers in four contrasting LEAs, reported considerable scepticism about inspection amongst both advisers and teachers. This seems to be partly because inspection was not seen as presenting a reliable picture of a school for monitoring purposes, but mostly because inspection was not seen as an effective tool for development. Moreover, he was able to find little evidence that the LEA responded in any way to inspection.

Advisers seemed to prefer to work singly, devoting themselves primarily to support and development and keeping the LEA informed of problems they might find in schools. Stillman and Grant (1989) and Heller (1988) suggested that there was no such thing as a typical adviser. Although they might, as Goodwin (1968) suggested, have carried the power of the LEA 'office' with them, their influence seems to have depended largely on their individual qualities and expertise. When they did visit schools together, it was as often to present a picture of 'good practice' for dissemination or to develop their own skills as it was to monitor. The third case study fitted this tradition of advisers working together to develop their skills. The Audit Commission (1989) reported that 19.9 per cent of inspection was for this purpose.

So, although there was some response from LEAs to the needs identified in 1976 for greater accountability, monitoring seems to have remained

quite a low priority over the next decade and inspection was generally reserved for emergencies. The sense that the profession should monitor itself
continued and was in some ways strengthened by the developments in school
self-evaluation.

Her Majesty's Inspectorate

While the LEAs used formal inspection infrequently, Her Majesty's Inspectors
(HMI) relied heavily on the team visitation. A DES document (1983) explained
that HM Inspectorate was professionally independent of government, LEAs
and teachers. The inspectors could 'report as they find, without fear or favour'.
Lawton (1988) suggested that HMI inspection had three main elements: 'check
on public funds; provision of information to the Secretary of State (eyes and
ears); provision of advice to schools (advisory)'.

HM Inspectorate has now been incorporated into Ofsted. Until the advent
of the Ofsted framework, HMIs did not use any published criteria. It could be
argued that they were inside their own 'secret garden'. They almost all had
a teaching background and they evaluated schools making judgements based
on 'connoisseurship'. Their work was often in the form of surveys, focusing
on one aspect, subject, or type of school. The reports of such surveys, such
as the *Aspects of Primary Education* series (HMI 1988–91) do partially reveal
what they were looking at and looking for.

The trend towards greater accountability was strengthened by the advent
of the Conservative government in 1979. HMI found it progressively more
difficult to retain their independence from the Department of Education and
Science (DES). In 1983 the Raynor Report (DES 1983) upheld the existence
of HMI but placed a stronger emphasis on 'standards' in their work. In that
year, HMI began to publish their reports.

Despite their use of implicit criteria, which Pearce (1986) was able to distil
into six key strands (plant, match, pedagogy, progression, professionalism,
and climate) HMI's long tradition of inspection did evolve into a tight set of
internal procedures. This gave rise to a very particular picture of what inspection involves, a kind of mythology, which I shall explore in more detail in
the next chapter.

Their style of inspection had a particularly judgemental feel. Their insistence that their judgements could not be challenged and their reporting on
the present state of a school, as opposed to whether it had developed or
declined over time, gave a hard edge to inspection which generated particular anxiety amongst those being inspected. This anxiety still features strongly
in inspection. Although Lawton suggested that HMI did offer advice, their
inspections were not necessarily seen in that light. Their advice tended to
come later, in the form of digests of their survey findings, or when they
offered courses. Their inspection reports contained 'recommendations' and
worked to the premise that it was not their responsibility to tell schools how
to carry out such recommendations.

This judgemental approach contrasted strongly with the LEA advisers' commitment to a more developmental emphasis. It is not surprising, as we shall

see in the next chapter, that teachers and headteachers have been somewhat confused about the judgemental and developmental mix when LEA advisers have engaged in more formal, HMI style, inspections. Pearce (1986) argued that HMI made it more difficult for LEA advisers to evolve coherent approaches to inspection. In the same year, a House of Commons Select Committee report, *Achievement in Primary Schools* (1986), argued that LEA advisers should undertake more inspection.

Lawton and Gordon (1987) point out that from 1979 onwards there was progressively stronger central government control of education. They identified three sets of ideologies: political, bureaucratic, and professional. They saw a strong political belief in the market, with an emphasis on the free choice of the buyer. At the same time, they noted the bureaucratic emphasis of the DES and its search for efficiency, particularly in administration, and its taste for performance indicators, particularly tests. HMI meanwhile were looking for professionalism and quality, favouring 'impressionistic evaluation' as their means of securing these values. These strands of ideology and control were brought into sharper focus by the Education Reform Act (1988) and will be further considered below.

Curriculum issues

Pearce (1986) argued that it was the curriculum vacuum which weakened accountability. Callaghan's 'secret garden' seems to have contained two key forms of vegetation – the curriculum and professionalism. The professionalism debate is discussed in Chapter 9. As for the curriculum, it has been, and remains, a political football. Without a consensus over what was to be taught, it was undoubtedly difficult to hold schools to account over how well it was taught. An early attempt to bring some control over the curriculum was the setting up of the Schools Council (1964). Ten years later the Assessment of Performance Unit (1974) was established to look closely at standards in the core subjects of English, mathematics and science. Nevertheless, controversy raged on. The 'Black Papers' of the late 1960s, contrasted with the alleged freedom of teachers 'to do whatever they want' at William Tyndale (1976) reveal the confusion. The primary curriculum was influenced to an extent by the secondary curriculum. This in turn was subject to the considerable control of the universities through the examination system. Even so, there was still room for the Schools Council's relatively radical Humanities Project, albeit intended primarily for young school leavers, alongside the more traditional history syllabi of dates and kings and queens.

During the 1980s, the government's Department of Education and Science sought to bring greater influence over the curriculum. It published guidance; but so did the Schools Council. HMI too published their series of *Curriculum Matters* documents (1985–9). The Education Act (1986) required LEAs to publish a curriculum statement and also required school governors to publish a school curriculum statement. However, although there was considerable consensus between these many different documents, the fact that the DES, the Schools Council, HMI, LEAs and governors were all seen to have a legitimate contribution to make demonstrates the range of interested parties.

The Education Reform Act (1988)

Despite these developments during the first eight or nine years of the Thatcher government, by 1988 the stage was set for a legislative bonanza. In a wider context of significant changes in the whole political and cultural landscape, the curriculum was still seen as in need of greater control; the power of the buyer was considered to be in need of enhancement; the power of many, particularly metropolitan, local education authorities had become inconvenient to central government; the teaching profession had been brought to heel following a substantial period of industrial action; and accountability was seen to be in need of strengthening, particularly in terms of efficiency and outcomes. The time to wrestle control of the educational agenda away from the secret garden of the professionals seemed ripe.

The Education Reform Act (1988) contained provisions to establish a National Curriculum, with an associated set of national assessment procedures. It also contained provisions to insist that LEAs delegated funds to the direct control of the schools themselves; to give schools the right to opt out of LEA control; and to give parents the right to choose which school they wanted for their children, through open enrolment.

The effect of this legislation on inspection was substantial. LEAs were to be responsible for monitoring the implementation of the National Curriculum. Although their patronage over the schools was undermined by the delegation of funds, there was an increasing call for them to monitor the use of public funds, particularly as the market ideology, with its emphasis on financial efficiency, was taking hold. The Audit Commission published its report *Assuring Quality in Education* (1989) which urged LEAs to increase their monitoring function:

> Assurance can come only as a result of professional monitoring, including direct observation (inspection). Measures to secure improvement also require a detached professional input (advice) (p. 1).

> The Audit Commission's interest in inspection and advisory services arises from its duty to address the effectiveness of local authorities' operations as well as their economy and efficiency. Successful work by the LEA's own services to promote quality is one of the most important contributions to ensuring the effectiveness of LEA-maintained education (p. 3).

In a climate where LEAs felt increasingly insecure, the response was for many of them to rename their advisers as inspectors and to set up authority-wide review cycles. Five of the case studies exemplify this.

HMI continued to inspect schools as before, but with a strong focus on the implementation of the National Curriculum. For a short period, until they were incorporated into Ofsted in 1992, HMI began to work more closely with

LEAs to develop the kind of inspection that the Audit Commission advocated. The growing emphasis on standards, which found its legislative realisation in the provisions for national assessment, was reflected in the tone of HMI reporting. In 1988, the HM Chief Inspector began to publish an annual report which summarised the findings of inspections across the country and identified trends in standards.

The Parent's Charter

The growing incidence of reporting progressively raised the stakes for those being inspected. This culminated in the publication, as part of the government's Citizen's Charter initiative, of the Parent's Charter in 1992. Parents would be entitled to information which would assist them in making choices in the educational market place. They would receive the results of standard assessments, there would be more performance indicators on attendance and truancy, and there would be league tables to compare the performance of one school with another. Following the 1992 Education Act, all of these figures had to be included in an inspection report and the report itself would provide a four-yearly quality check on each and every school.

The 1992 Education Act itself fitted firmly into the context of the Parent's Charter. One of its special provisions was that inspection teams must contain a 'lay' inspector. The rationale for this appears to be that someone untainted by professional training will provide a more accessible, common-sense, view of what is taking place within the school which will help to provide an insight for the parent as consumer. A further Education Act in 1993 tightened the provisions of inspection by spelling out the consequences for a school which does not meet the expectations of the Ofsted inspectors. Such schools will be accorded 'special measures' which might include LEA support, or support from a specially formed group called an 'education association', or might ultimately entail closure by the Secretary of State.

Ideologies

Several different groups of stakeholders are affected by inspections and these groups may have conflicting ideologies. Between 1976 and 1994 there appears to have been a political shift in emphasis towards a market ideology, with the parent as consumer, at the expense of a professional ideology, where teachers had effective control over what they taught as well as how they taught it. However, as will become apparent, the professional ideology still occupies a significant position in inspections. Although teachers have felt that their professionalism has been under scrutiny, some teachers have found that inspection has helped them to define their professional commitment more clearly. Inspectors have certainly been motivated by the idea of 'doing a professional job', in which they appear to have felt answerable to each other and to the teachers they have been inspecting as much as they have to any other clients for their work.

However, although it is difficult to chart shifts in values from within an ideology, it must be conceded that what is valued now by professionals may not have quite the same emphasis as it did in 1976. The notion of standards has moved closer to the centre of the stage and there has been a growing recognition that the quality of teaching cannot be judged other than by looking at the quality of the learning taking place. But, as is discussed in the next chapter, teachers do not seem to have accepted the parent as their client – their accountability seems to be to their peers, or towards the child, or to the school itself, or to a sense of personal pride, and sometimes, though infrequently, to the governors.

Whilst politically the government may have been attempting to undermine – perhaps even to manipulate – the LEAs, a majority of the newly accredited Ofsted inspectors has come from the LEAs. The procedures and the implicit criteria of HMI have now been shared with LEA personnel, perhaps distancing the focus of this expertise away from government and towards the LEA professional. There has been considerable concern in the press that LEA inspectors will dominate the Ofsted inspection market and that, in many cases, they will be inspecting schools in their own LEA.

Along the way, inspection procedures have become rather more technical. The centrality of judgement nevertheless remains paramount. The evaluation criteria offered by the Framework for Inspection are now explicit, but they are still qualitative not quantitative. The use of the term 'impressionistic' still applies, but the careful recording of evidence and the use of grades, which can be quantitatively accumulated, might be seen to place the 'connoisseurship' analogy with wine or tea tasting within a more 'objective' context. Nevertheless, the early experience of lay inspectors suggests that inspection is difficult for those who do not have a professional background in schools and Ofsted itself will not accept tenders for inspections which give lay inspectors any lead responsibility to make judgements about standards in subjects. Becher's (1978: 225) distinction between process and product, analogous to running and completing a race, makes it difficult for the lay person: 'Process requires relatively informal methods. The emphasis is on credibility and accessibility. It shares the relativity of any transaction between professional and client.'

Anthea Millett (1992), when Director of Inspection at Ofsted, claimed that the framework for inspection represents 'an outcomes-driven model of inspection'. This could, in Lawton and Gordon's terms, suggest that it fits more closely to a bureaucratic ideology. Millett's assertion reflects the intention that judgements be made on the basis of whether teaching is working, rather than on the substance of the teaching itself, ends rather than means. But this is hardly the approach of the office-based administrator, based on quantitative data, performance indicators, and testing. It still requires observation and judgement to make the assessment, let alone the judgement required to interpret it. Nevertheless, the professional perspective has been sharpened by the bureaucratic ideology, partly through this shift towards ends over means, but particularly through the inclusion of 'efficiency' as a core consideration in the framework. Inspectors now have to make 'a summative assessment of the value for money provided by the school' (p. 21).

Perhaps the significance of inspection will be undermined eventually by the search for 'bureaucratic' indicators of value added. Thus far, league tables comparing the results of national assessments, whilst they have undoubtedly focused minds, have raised a host of difficult questions about accuracy and fairness. The teachers' unions have resisted the publication of test results except at 16+, and other quantitative indicators – such as those for attendance – only address tangential issues. Nevertheless, the search for value-added indicators continues, with considerable interest in 'base-line' assessment at 4+ or 5+. The Ofsted, professional, opinion is that quantitative indicators need the additional explanation of observational assessment. It is difficult to see how this professional opinion could be totally displaced, but it is almost as difficult to comprehend the extent to which professional accountability has changed over a 20-year period. If inspection were eventually to be sidelined by quantitative indicators, the significant cost of establishing the complex Ofsted system could prove to be something of an embarrassment.

The first of the three ideologies identified by Lawton and Gordon (1987) was a political ideology which currently manifests itself as that of the market and free choice. This ideology affects inspection in that the inspection report can be used to inform the parent-consumer as choices are made between schools. This raises the stakes considerably for the teachers, headteacher and governors of the school being inspected and raises the spectre of litigation should inspectors fail to underpin their judgements with cast-iron evidence.

Lawton and Gordon's suggestion that inspection is part of a market ideology is related to an increased emphasis on managerialism since the installation of the Conservative government in 1979. Stillman and Grant (1989: 86) note that there has been 'a move away from amateurism towards management'. Winkley (1985: 19) asks where the inspector fits into a triangle of 'efficiency, educational excellence and democracy' without offering a clear answer but with the suggestion that, at least in some LEAs, the inspector acts on behalf of management. He referred to the 'new managerialism' rather dismissively, suggesting that quality control was replacing any real idea about how quality might grow. This resonates with a comment made by an inspector in one of the case studies who commented that 'nothing grows just by measuring it'. Although this comment might have some truth at the level of the individual institution, it is difficult to dispute the improvements that have occurred as a result of comparative league tables and a greater emphasis on comparative standards.

Henkel (1991) made comparisons between the Audit Commission, the Social Services Inspectorate and the Health Advisory Service in order to illustrate a thesis that the impact of evaluation is congruent with the dominant political ideology of the day. She showed how the values of the evaluators are derived from occupational or disciplinary traditions and pointed up the sharp contrast between two views of management – the technical and the human. She suggested that the technical view was more typical of the Audit Commission, with its emphases on economy, efficiency and effectiveness. The human view was most typical of the Health Advisory Service, with its emphasis on professional judgement. The Social Services Inspectorate, which originally had a more advisory culture, has moved towards technical management. In doing so, Henkel suggested that it had gained greater credibility with government.

Henkel's argument seems to have been borne out by what has happened in education. The inclusion of 'efficiency' in the Ofsted framework has moved inspection in a distinctly technical direction. Interestingly, the government's preoccupation with spiritual and moral issues in education, perhaps at its strongest during John Patten's tenure as Secretary of State for Education, has simultaneously pushed inspection in the opposite direction.

Henkel's analysis of the relationship between evaluation agencies and government questioned expectations that evaluators might affect the decision-making of government. Instead, she argued that the government makes evaluation its agent of change. Insofar as teachers have said that inspection has helped them to define their professional obligations, we can see how the formulation and the use of the Ofsted framework for inspection match her argument. Nevertheless, the general messiness within the processes and outcomes of inspection suggests that evaluation may be rather imprecise as an agent of change.

A good example of evaluation as an agent of change is the shift in the role of governors. Since the legislation of 1986, the powers of governors have increased substantially and the delegation of funding since 1988 has intensified their responsibilities. However, prior to the implementation of Ofsted procedures, the governors, whilst receiving privileged access to any inspection findings, appear generally to have been able to remain detached from inspections taking place in their schools. This remained true even in case studies where the inspection report was published. Now, under the Ofsted procedures governors are officially required to formulate an action plan following an Ofsted inspection. If such an action plan were to involve the competence of the headteacher, the governors would be forced to act. Although it is still the case that many governing bodies submit an action plan which has been formulated on their behalf by the headteacher, there can be no doubt that Ofsted inspection has begun to enforce the obligations of the 1986 Act.

Thus far, there are few who have researched or written about the involvement of governors either within inspections or as an audience. A considerable amount has been written to explain Ofsted inspection to governors, but there has been little systematic exploration of the relationship between governors and inspection except in occasional references in the educational press to criticism of governors by Ofsted inspectors.

We shall see in the case studies how the changes in ideology and culture over the past 20 years or so surface in the perceptions of inspectors, headteachers, teachers, and some governors. Of the 12 cases, two were conducted by HMI under the full provisions of the Ofsted framework; two were pilot Ofsted inspections undertaken by LEA teams; five were LEA inspections undertaken in the context of an authority-wide review programme; one was an inspection undertaken by an LEA team essentially for its own training purposes; and two were inspections undertaken by LEA teams for 'special reasons'. It is important to recognise that the experience of inspection has been, until now, an uncommon one. Few LEAs undertook authority-wide inspection before 1988 and HMI were only ever able to inspect between 1 and 2% of schools in any one year.

It will be for others to look at the system-wide aspects of inspection, to attempt to ascertain how well inspection serves the interests of the Parent's Charter, whether or not it has exposed the secrets of the 'secret garden', and whether it has strengthened or weakened the LEA's position. This book focuses particularly on two sets of stakeholders – the inspectors and the teachers. The significance of this general discussion about the culture of inspection lies in the extent to which conflicting perceptions might complicate the processes or outcomes of inspections for these two particular groups of people.

2 EXPECTATIONS AND

PRECONCEPTIONS

This chapter explores the expectations and preconceptions that headteachers, teachers, governors and inspectors have of inspection. Two important themes emerge: a tension between judgement for accountability and judgement for development; and the mythology of inspection. In both of these themes, the strong personal and emotional impact of inspection becomes apparent.

One of the questions that I pursued in my research interviews was about the purposes of the particular inspection we were talking about. I had assumed at the outset of the project that teachers would have clear expectations of purposes. Were this so, it would have been possible to ask them to consider whether these purposes had been achieved and whether there were particular aspects of the inspection's processes which seemed to have either helped or hindered such achievement. I was also interested to discover the inspectors' perceptions of their purposes. I knew, from my own experience of inspecting in schools where there were particular difficulties, that inspectors sometimes had agendas, particularly if there were concerns about the management of the school, which could not easily be shared. I was interested to discover whether any mismatch of perception about purposes and expectations made a difference.

As it has turned out, my initial assumption that teachers and inspectors would have clear views about purposes proved to be unsound. The culture of inspection contains several strands, as we have seen in the previous chapter, and it seems to have been unrealistic to expect clear formulations of purpose, particularly when people were still very close to the experience of the inspection itself. Nevertheless, purposes have emerged, as have some evident mismatches between inspectors' purposes and teachers' perceptions of those purposes. At the same time, there have been several instances where teachers found it difficult to identify a clear purpose or recall that they had been told of any by the inspectors. On one level, such teachers do not appear to have been worried by this, since there appears to have been a stronger need for teachers to know *what* was going to happen than *why*, and also there has been a tendency for teachers to subject themselves to inspection rather passively. On another level, it has been possible to see that, had there been a clearer understanding of purposes, some of the complaints or confusions voiced by teachers might have been avoided and there might have been less resistance to what inspectors did or said.

Judgemental or developmental?

In considering the purposes of inspection, teachers talked of being 'checked up on'; of inspectors wanting 'to help move the school on'; of 'being accountable'; of inspectors using 'the school as an example of good practice'; of inspectors wanting 'to see whether we were coping with the National Curriculum'; of being 'kept on our toes'; and of the value of 'an outside view'. This sample of comments identifies the main strands of purpose which surfaced. The inspectors' responses generated a similar range of purposes. Running through these purposes there is a tension between judgements being made for themselves and judgements being used for development. Sometimes there was also a sense of judgements being used punitively.

This tension, between what I shall refer to as the 'judgemental' position and the 'developmental' position, is similar to that which exists when children are assessed, particularly since the advent of a statutory assessment framework in the 1988 Education 'Reform' Act. When children are assessed at the end of a National Curriculum key stage, perhaps with the aid of 'standard assessment tasks' (SATs), the idea is to validate the learning which has so far taken place. The judgements are used 'summatively' to sum up the progress made. At the same time, assessment is usually intended to identify what children next need to do and to learn. When assessment is used in this way, it is helping to 'form' the subsequent curriculum – this is 'formative' assessment.

In the course of this and subsequent chapters, I shall use the terms 'judgemental' and 'developmental' to express this difference. The terms 'summative' and 'formative' could be seen as more appropriate since they avoid any suggestion that judgement is not common to both situations. I have elected to use the more user-friendly, less jargonised, terms. 'Judgemental' does carry a sense of 'sitting in judgement', which matches the way that many teachers have conceptualised and experienced inspection. The important point to understand is that the term 'judgemental' is intended to imply judgement *for itself,* underpinned by the idea of validation of existing or previous performance, whereas 'developmental' is intended to suggest that judgement is being seen as a means to the improvement of future performance.

The purely judgemental expectation – accountability

Teachers in almost every case have alluded to the idea of an assessment of the school's current performance: 'to report on the school's standing – what it says and what is actually happening'.

This perception, which was put forward in a case which preceded the advent of the Ofsted framework, suggested that the inspectors' judgements would be based on the school's own intentions. It was matched by one of the inspection team who suggested that he was trying 'to find out how the school arrived at its perceptions of quality'. In another pre-framework case, one of the inspectors likened the inspection to a 'health check – like the medical model'. As people adjusted to the existence of the Ofsted framework, 'standards' were seen increasingly frequently as part of the inspection agenda: 'they want to see appropriate standards'.

Besides standards and quality, the other specific focus of judgemental inspection often mentioned was the National Curriculum: 'There's surely got to be someone who monitors the National Curriculum!' It was perhaps surprising how often teachers referred to inspectors wanting to 'provide an objective picture of the school' or their 'assessing the school to see whether it is doing what it ought to be' without indicating any sense of accountability beyond the inspection team, even when the report was to be published.

There was a significant number of teachers who seemed to see inspection in these purely judgemental terms. They conceded, rather reluctantly, that 'there has to be an element of judgement about it', and one teacher commented ruefully that 'we do not enjoy the prospect of being judged'. This resistance to judgement was directly linked with the sense of being victims of inspection and with their high levels of anxiety. It may also have stemmed from a misunderstanding of the place of judgement in a more developmental agenda which is itself linked to perceptions of 'advisers' when they are involved in inspection.

The resistance to judgement was not limited to this group who had the purely judgemental perception of inspection. There were many who were able to link judgement with an awareness that the inspectors were agents of a wider accountability. Common to all these teachers was the tendency to take inspection personally.

Even teachers who were well aware that it was the school which was being inspected articulated a strong sense of personal accountability. One teacher 'made sure to my satisfaction that my nose was clean'; another said, 'you are putting yourself on the line'. This personalisation was sometimes related to the school: 'As an NQT, I was used to having people observe me. But the fact that I'd be accountable to the school made a difference. My performance could affect the whole school.' Sometimes it was more directly related to promotion: 'Would a bad day affect your career?'

In the small school, the sense of personal vulnerability was hardly surprising: 'You can't have anonymity in small schools.' However, sometimes teachers conceded that their expectation of personal exposure was misplaced: 'It was less individual than I'd expected.' And sometimes the personalisation of the inspection experience was more positive and developmental: 'I saw the inspection in very personal terms – as a learning opportunity.'

This comment heralds the more developmental agenda of many teachers and of all the inspectors. Before exploring this in more detail, we should look more closely at accountability which, from the teachers' standpoint, seems to have been experienced more judgementally than developmentally. The fact that the preoccupation of some teachers with their personal performance seems to have made it difficult for them to look beyond the inspectors did not prevent others from recognising that the inspection had a wider purpose:

'At the end of the day we have to be accountable to someone – in the interests of the children.'

'The inspectors were reporting up the line.'

'It was an accountability exercise – the education committee has to be seen to be monitoring the schools in their care.'

'Parents have a right to know.'

'It's a check by the LEA of a sample of schools – random quality control.'

'The county is responsible – they need to know if a school is not functioning properly.'

'I'm accountable to the county.'

'It's for the betterment of the system of the country, though I feel accountable to the children.'

'We're accountable to parents.'

'It would put us on a league table.'

All of these comments, apart from the last one, came from class teachers. It was a headteacher who mentioned league tables; otherwise headteachers focused particularly on their accountability to their own LEA. Again, apart from the last comment, these responses did not relate to inspections which were undertaken using the Ofsted framework. In the four case studies which did use the framework, two HMI inspections and two LEA pilot inspections, teachers did not nominate an external agency to whom they were accountable. Instead they referred to standards or to the National Curriculum – the purely judgemental position – or they talked of accountability to the school or to the children. In all four of these cases, there was a stronger sense of the teachers as victims; perhaps because the stakes were higher because of the new framework and because, in two of these cases, a report was to be published externally. The newness of the Ofsted approach may also have meant that they were less clear about the lines of accountability involved.

Governors did not feature as a focus for teacher accountability. An inspector commented: 'Teachers don't feel accountable towards governors – to the head and senior management, yes, and to inspectors and advisers, though in a different way. Even parents don't often feature on the list.'

Teachers mentioned governors just twice in the context of accountability: 'I'm accountable to the head. The head is accountable to the education officer and to the governors. In theory I am accountable to the governors but this is faintly ridiculous. You need to be accountable to people who know what they are doing.' This is not necessarily a typical perception of governors although the other mention was only a little more positive: 'The governors showed an interest but they didn't really know what was happening.'

It would appear that the governors' position in relation to inspection is anomalous. They are simultaneously inside and outside the inspection. One governor pointed out that 'governors need to know – because of their part in decision-making' but quickly went on to explain that the LEA 'needs an outside view – they need to know how well our school is doing'. She spoke with a sense of detachment which was illustrated by her comment that the inspectors had 'hoped that we might have some tales to tell'. This suggested that the governors were being treated as a source of information about the school, rather than as part of the school being inspected. This was an LEA review. The governors in an HMI inspection seemed similarly detached, even when the lead inspector presented some unpalatable findings. They did not appear to recognise the implications of the impending publication of the report. Now that the cycle of Ofsted inspection is fully established, this picture is changing, but slowly.

The picture of accountability given by the teachers and the headteachers, in the context of the case studies, is a fragmented one. There are several possible explanations for this: Firstly, we have been considering external accountability, which excludes any sense of accountability to one's own professionalism. Professional accountability has proved to be a significant feature in the case studies.

Secondly, it may well be that teachers do not have a strong sense of accountability to more remote players in the system. They acknowledge the existence of their LEA, with whom there can be some identification, but there is no particular reason why they should be concerned with the political structures which lie behind inspectors. Their preoccupation is more likely to be with the direct impact of the inspection than with considerations of why inspection is there.

Thirdly, teachers have articulated a sense of accountability closer to their immediate workplace. Parents have been mentioned, and children have featured relatively strongly: 'We're mostly accountable to the children we teach.' One inspector commented: 'Teachers seem to feel accountable to the head, it's a kind of loyalty.'

Although this kind of accountability, to the school, or the headteacher, or both, has rarely been explicit, it has implicitly pervaded all the interviews.

The inspectors' view of accountability again proved to be more internal than external overall and was not significantly clearer. Externally, inspectors have talked of 'a veiled threat that HMI would come if we didn't [a political accountability where the 'we' refers to inspectors as representatives of the LEA]'; 'We were there for the County Council. It is our responsibility to keep the purseholders of the community informed'; 'The report does go to the CEO'; 'The LEA has a monitoring role under the 1988 Act.'

They have also alluded to governors, but more in the operational context of feeding back to them than in terms of accountability. However, one inspector said 'I'm accountable to the head and the governors – and to myself. I don't have the school in my mind's eye (when I write the report). It is the governors I have in mind.'

This single reference to governors in the context of accountability also, by referring to the head and to 'myself', reveals the prevalence of a more internal accountability. Another inspector, in emphasising the developmental aspect of inspection dismissed the accountability to the county as 'really an irrelevance'. This was echoed: 'The county has to be seen to know what is happening in their schools; the official audience is the elected members. But the school as a whole is the unofficial audience. Individual advisers would want to have sufficient personal power to subvert the aim and make it a positive experience.'

As inspectors talked about the real audiences for their reports, referring at times to 'clients', the orientation of their accountability seemed to move inwards:

'I was writing for the subject consultant. The report isn't really for the governors.'

'There doesn't seem to be any reaction or response from the LEA to a report.'

'It's a problem writing for the county council but wanting it to work at the school level.'

'We have an accountability towards the staff.'

'I have the teachers and the head in my mind's eye when I'm writing.'

'Ultimately it's for the children – I get angry when they aren't getting a fair deal.'

'I'm not sure if it's the head or the teachers I write for. I do try to check it out for other audiences but I'm not sure I'm very good at that.'

'My accountability is to myself – I like to do the job properly.'

'I feel accountable to the school, to the team, to my own professional expectations of myself.'

'My accountability is for myself – I've got to live with myself and then with others, especially the school. The audience for the report is the school – and then Ofsted.'

'I'm accountable to myself initially – the school, the pupils, colleagues, not to Ofsted or the government – perhaps to our senior management.'

We can see in this selection of comments that the notion of 'accountability' is complex. Becher and Eraut (1982) identify three 'facets' of accountability: moral accountability, by which one is answerable to one's clients; contractual accountability, by which one is accountable to one's employers and political masters; and professional accountability, by which one is responsible to oneself and to one's colleagues. A fourth kind of accountability has been alluded to in the previous chapter: market accountability. This could be seen as a combination of contractual and moral accountability.

Eraut (1992: 19) talks of 'professional' accountability as including:

• a moral commitment to serve the interests of clients;
• a professional obligation to self-monitor and periodically to review the effectiveness of one's practice;
• a professional obligation to expand one's repertoire, to reflect on one's experience and to develop one's expertise;
• an obligation that is professional as well as contractual to contribute to the quality of one's organisation;
• an obligation to reflect on and contribute to discussions on the changing role of one's profession in a wider society.

Several of the comments of both inspectors and teachers begin to fit these expectations. There is moral accountability towards the child-client and, for inspectors, the teacher-client, although this is not as strong a feature of people's preoccupations with professionalism as we might expect. We shall see (in Chapter 9) how the whole process of inspection might be seen as a contribution to the second and third of Eraut's points. We can also see vestiges of contractual accountability in inspectors' references to the LEA (their employers) and to 'senior management'.

As well as these types or 'facets' of accountability, the comments of teachers and inspectors have revealed the clients or 'constituencies' (Sockett 1980) of accountability, such as the child, colleagues, the parent, governors, or the LEA. Pearce (1986) explores the idea of whether these different types or clients of accountability form a hierarchy. He suggests that a 'network' might be a more appropriate organising principle. This may be true in relation to less well-defined constituencies, or influences, such as the press or the community. However, the pattern of responses in the research interviews suggests that there is a hierarchy of the types of accountability. The anxiety and personalisation associated with inspection by the least secure teachers would be about contractual accountability, particularly when associated with any real or mythological punitive consequences. The 'irrelevance' of the paymaster expressed by some would indicate a greater level of professional security allowing teachers or inspectors to move away – upwards – from contractual accountability towards moral or professional accountability.

This would account for a swing towards a more developmental agenda which was frequently articulated. The purely judgemental agenda, linked with an external, more contractual, kind of accountability could be said to have a minimalist feel. So the school is to be assessed – so what?

This matches the idea, expressed by one inspector, that 'nothing grows just by measuring it'. In actuality, the bio-logic of this comment is misleading when transferred to a different context. The publication of assessments can have an effect on subsequent action, as has been well demonstrated by the pressure on standards which has been exerted by the league tables for examination results at 16+. Sockett (1982: 10) links the holding of people to account with 'an attempt to improve the quality of education'. He also links it to 'proof that this is being done' (p. 40). Pearce (1986) also asserts that accountability must be seen to happen.

This latter point also illustrates the idea of 'market' accountability. The Ofsted framework outlines the purpose of inspection as follows: 'to identify strengths and weaknesses in schools so that they may improve the quality of education offered and raise the standards achieved by their pupils. The publication of the report and summary report of the inspection of a school is consistent with the requirements of the Parent's Charter.'

Teachers made a few references to the visibility of inspection: 'it has to be seen to be done'; 'they needed to be seen to be doing their job'. This is still essentially an external aspect of accountability. It could be seen as related to contractual accountability, since the Parent's Charter could be construed as a kind of contract, albeit one which teachers had little part in signing. As consumers, parents do affect the number of pupils in the school and so, particularly since they are also taxpayers, they might be described as paymasters.

Market accountability requires visibility – it must be accessible to the consumer. This could be seen ideologically as a replacement for local democratic accountability, by which the voter would make decisions about, say, the performance of a local council. Winkley (1985: 19) asks 'what is the proper relationship between efficiency, educational excellence and democracy? – and where does the inspector fit into this triangle?' Efficiency is now incorporated into the inspection framework. Since the inspection itself is an evaluation of educational excellence, the democratic requirement is then met by the visibility of the inspection through the publication of its report.

Might there be any other reason why teachers should assert that inspectors need to be seen in action? After all, their familiarity with accountability does not seem to have been particularly sophisticated. It is possible that validation, which proves to be significant as an outcome of inspection, is strengthened if it is public. On the other hand, if teachers wanted any validation of their practice to be publicised, it would conflict with their emotional response. The anxiety of inspection is significantly increased when the inspectors' judgements are put on public record.

The developmental expectation

The link between an account of a school's strengths and weaknesses and improvement, promoted by the Ofsted framework and asserted by Sockett, is echoed by several commentators and researchers on inspection, accountability and evaluation. Bolam *et al.* (1978: 81) suggested that 'inspection gives sufficient authority to encourage teachers to look more critically at the situation';

Marjoram (1989: 16), conceding that his argument is rational not definitional, claimed that 'assessment *should* promote action for improvement', and suggested that 'assessment can ipso facto generate new ideas'; Beeby (1977: 22), defining educational evaluation, talked of 'the systematic collection and interpretation of evidence leading, as part of the process, to a judgement of value with a view to action'; and McCormick and James (1983) maintained that inspection implies both judgement and development.

There are probably more commentators in this field who would be sceptical of a link between accountability or external evaluation and improvement. Much of this scepticism hinges on some aspect of ownership. Their argument would be that any change which follows inspection is likely to be, at best, skin deep, since inspection is coercive and too quick. So Schön (1987) talked of being a 'parrot', Eraut (1978) talked of 'token adoption', and Alexander (1991) talked of 'strategic compliance'. Biott and Nias (1992) argued that change is organic and that it needs to be voluntary, informal and sustained; they would not have associated these conditions with inspection. MacDonald (1978: 130) argued that: 'the adviser rendering evaluative summaries . . . cannot function credibly as an external auditor without severely curtailing (to put it mildly) the collaborative role of the adviser. It is a heavy price to pay for accountability.'

Becher (1978: 221) pointed out that there has not been 'much evidence to suggest that performance auditing can lead to identifiable improvements in practice'. Winkley (1985: 11) echoed this: 'There is no evident relation between inspectorial visits and the excellence of schools.'

The teachers involved in the cases that I researched often had a more positive expectation of inspection as a formative influence:

'We need to feel that we can get something out of it.'

'They look at what we're doing well and find areas for development.'

'Inspectors are critical friends – they should have a direct interest in improvement.'

'They will expect us to draw up an action plan from their recommendations.'

'I hope the professional view is to go beyond accountability to give some structure to support the school forwards.'

However, these more positive expectations do not necessarily refute the scepticism of commentators. Several headteachers had gone out of their way to engender a positive spirit amongst their staffs in advance of the inspection. We may have evidence of positive expectation but this does not provide evidence that the expectations were or would be fulfilled.

Inspectors voiced their expectations of a link between inspection and development more strongly:

'The aim is to benefit the pupils.'

'It is an unwritten assumption that recommendations will follow a review; it will be difficult for the head not to take them forward.'

'The report will provide pressure for the school to act on our recommendations.'

'It will focus development and probably, through its professional credibility or through the stick of the published report, secure a will to work on the foci.'

'It has a developmental purpose – the report can be used as an *aide-mémoire* in the future.'

'The developmental aspect must come out of the inspection.'

'I'd expect the school to act on our comments.'

'Inspection is to try to improve quality in the classroom.'

'I did not want to leave them worse off than we had found them.'

Again we have the difficulty that an expectation of development does not necessarily secure it. There was a strong sense of wish-fulfilment in the comments of inspectors. This may have reflected the shifting culture which had recently moved many of the inspectors out of a more purely advisory role. The scepticism of commentators about the developmental impact of inspection often applied to advisers as well but, insofar as advisers had convinced themselves that their advisory work did have a positive impact, there was sometimes a feeling that they were wanting to convince themselves that inspection would be similarly worthwhile.

In the earlier case studies, adviser-inspectors were still identifying themselves as advisers: 'advisers don't like inspecting'. This whole issue of whether inspection is developmental has, throughout the project, been strongly bound up with the legacy of the advisory culture. In the second case study, there was an interesting shift which one of the inspectors explained: 'There are two ways in which an inspection can go. You can have an explicit focus, criteria crystal clear. You report back directly on the evidence seen and your professional judgements. Or, you can find yourself in a school inspecting, you think the climate is receptive and you try to get the staff involved in the inspection themselves. The one is a clipboard exercise, the other is not. There is a decision point about which kind of an inspection it should be.'

This approach was not representative of the other case studies. Nevertheless it illustrates some of the tensions between inspection and advice. The kind of inspection experienced in most of the case studies was this inspector's first version, though not always with clear criteria. It was about evidence and judgement. Yet, lurking behind the work of several of the inspectors and behind the expectations of several teachers, was the desire to move into a more collaborative exchange. It may be a moot point as to whether such exchanges achieved more development, but they would at least have been more palatable on a human level.

In this case study, the teachers were happy to talk about the inspectors 'making suggestions' for them to try out. In a later case study, which took place 20 months later, one of the inspectors was saying: 'I stick to the inspector role. Teachers get confused by a lot of suggestions.' Certainly, an out-of-place suggestion about cushions in one case did go quite a long way towards undermining the credibility of the inspector concerned.

Along the way, the distinction between adviser and inspector surfaced quite frequently. In one case study, a teacher reported that the inspectors had 'stressed that they weren't here in an advisory capacity'. Nevertheless, one of the inspectors said that 'whatever came out, they'd expect me to help them take it on'. Another inspector saw that 'under section 9 [Ofsted] inspection, the school would look for consultancy', clearly seeing herself as such a consultant. A third inspector emphasised that 'we offer support, not advice'; 'we can give an opinion, but we are not into cloning'. She pointed out that 'advisers should extend, not diminish, the role of the head – it is not for us to take on the role of the head.' Even so, she revealed that the team had offered staff 'a chance to talk to the advisers as consultants, in private' during the inspection. In other cases, one inspector conceded that 'I want to advise as I inspect – the schools want help to solve the problems we identify', while another 'found it difficult not to move into a position of advice' and another said he 'can't see a conflict between inspector and adviser'.

There does appear to have been, if not a conflict, at least a mismatch of expectations about inspectors moving into a position of advice. The comments refer to two sets of issues: dialogue during the inspection, and follow-up afterwards. Teachers' perceptions of the 'fairness' of inspections may affect their validity. One teacher felt that 'it would have been fairer if they had given us a chance to ask them things we want to know – these people were advisers.'

This was a plea for dialogue during the inspection. In another case a teacher had liked the opportunities they had had 'to ask them to put on another hat and give us some suggestions. It would have been good if there could have been more of that.' It would seem that 'advice' in the context of an inspection occurred when an inspector went beyond judgement to the point of making suggestions: 'He did say you ought to try this and that – he was more of an adviser.'

Yet, inspectors did make recommendations. The distinction seems to have been between identifying an issue which the school 'ought' to address, and giving the school ways in which to address the issue.

The idea of offering consultancy after the inspection would keep the advisory mode separate from the inspection itself. At the same time, it raises questions about whether this implies that inspection itself would not contribute to development without the advisory follow-up. Certainly one inspector was clear about this: 'If we don't go back to follow it up, it will have been a waste of time.'

Follow-up was widely expected. One teacher asked: 'They identified J— [a colleague] as needing help – what are they going to do about it?' An inspector asked: 'Do I have any business there if I can't guarantee follow-up support?' In this case, the distinction between suggestions during an inspection and follow-up afterwards became very clear in rather heated exchanges when the inspectors fed back to the staff: 'The staff said, "it's all right making suggestions, but how are we going to be enabled?" Our suggestions rebounded on us.'

It appeared in one case that the credibility of the inspectors was enhanced by the fact that 'they do follow things through' – referring to how these inspectors had followed up inspections in other schools. In another case, there was a deliberate relationship between the inspection and the role of the LEA's 'link advisers': 'Schools will use the link adviser for follow-up, part of the agenda is to see where we can help inform the link adviser role.' This is the relationship which is now formalised under the Ofsted procedures. The school cannot be inspected by an inspector who has a previous connection with it. The Ofsted team would feed information to those who might subsequently support the school.

A polarity of a kind between judgement and development seems to emerge from the data. Even the National Association for Inspectors, Educational Advisers and Consultants (NAIEAC), reviewing a National Foundation for Educational Research (NFER) study by Maychell and Keys (1993) says that inspectors 'will wish to be clear in their own minds whether they are engaged in a judgemental or developmental process.'

I do not intend, at this stage, to attempt to resolve the question of whether inspection is, or is not, developmental. I will ultimately be questioning whether this polarity needs to be seen in oppositional terms, or whether the judgemental assessment cannot also be used diagnostically for developmental purposes. I will also be looking to see, in the light of the outcomes described by teachers, headteachers and inspectors, whether inspection can be linked directly with professional development. Coleman and Larocque (1990), looking at the evaluation of school districts in British Columbia, make an important distinction between the 'instrumental' use of data for 'direct action' and the 'conceptual' use of data for 'increased insight'. This distinction may prove helpful when we come to look more closely at the relationship between the inspection process and its outcomes. Meanwhile, the judgement–development polarity is a theme which we should bear in mind during the next few chapters. It is a theme which often recurs, and which helps to inform some of the perceptions of the participants in the case studies.

The shadow of myth

Teachers, and occasionally inspectors, have often revealed strong preconceptions about what inspection will involve, based sometimes on previous experience but more often on hearsay. A kind of myth has emerged which shows inspection as resembling some kind of archetypal monster.

Moore (1992) describes a myth as 'a sacred story set in a time and place outside history, describing in fictional form the fundamental truths of nature and human life' (p. 220). To place inspection into such a context rather overstates its significance. However, he goes on to say that 'Myth is always a way of imagining; it is not concerned essentially with fact' (p. 222).

The mythology of inspection seems to be concerned with this imagination. Teachers seem repeatedly to have been trying to make sense of the whole idea of inspection. It has carried the power to hurt and, less often, to heal, and has certainly touched their deeper sense of professional identity. In the midst of the day-to-day immediacy of managing classes of children, inspection seems to have raised difficult questions about what is expected and about who is in control.

We can begin to see how the myth has grown and how the monster has been fed. In the case studies, there were two sets of previous experience which were directly reported: 'In London I'd had an inspection – they ripped the school apart.' In the other situation, the headteacher related how 'bruised' certain members of his staff had been in a previous inspection. He had set out to 'protect' these staff at the outset of the inspection I was researching.

This sort of experience was then reported second-hand: 'one of the staff had had an unfortunate experience of inspection in a previous school'; 'T— was very hurt last time – she needed to be looked after'. This could build on itself, to the point where an inspector found this: 'There was frequent mention of a previous inspection which had made the staff feel very low. It had been built into the folklore – inspectors were a bad thing because people had suffered in the past. In actual fact, there were very few of the original staff still there.'

This 'folklore' contained stereotypical views of inspectors: as 'hit men'; 'the word "inspector" carries a picture'; 'I had a stereotype beforehand of starchy people'; 'I'd imagined they'd be trying to catch us out'; 'standing at the door with a stopwatch – that's the traditional view'. These teachers' comments reveal that any stereotype which existed was hardly positive; it is easy to see how the levels of anxiety were raised by the prospect of inspection.

Inspectors seemed well aware of the stereotypes: 'There's a them and us thing which comes from a general understanding of what an inspector, with a capital "i" is. You come in, look, be highly critical and go away. Inspection has connotations. It comes from rumour and an understanding of the HMI model. It is more threatening than the expectation of support you might get from an adviser.'

This inspector pointed the finger at the 'HMI model', revealing that the mythology may be more complex than a simple 'them and us' between teachers and inspectors. Might there not also have been a 'them and us' between this inspector (ex-adviser) and HMI? Another inspector said: 'teachers are amazed that we don't sit in a corner with a clipboard – it comes from HMI.' Pearce (1986) reinforces this demonisation of HMI. He suggests, alluding to them, tongue in cheek, as 'Her Majesty's pamphleteers', that they may have a greater influence on the schools they do not assess than those they do. Among the limitations of HMI inspection he lists, he includes teachers' perceptions of HMI inspection as 'a come-and-go service'. These comments could as easily be directed at Ofsted inspectors.

Later on we shall see that the mythology of inspection is a living tradition: the cases contained enough nightmarish experience to make their own contribution to it. The inspectors can add to the Chinese whispers unwittingly: one inspector, trying to reassure teachers at a pre-inspection briefing, outlined several of the stereotypes in her description of how the inspection was not going to take place. Her fierce manner seems only to have succeeded in confirming the teachers' worst fears. If another inspector had recounted to teachers that 'there are horror stories about inspectors going through teachers' desks' as he did during the research interview, the same thing might have occurred.

Another manifestation of inspection myth was the nightmare-that-might-have-been. So one teacher pointed out: 'we've never had poor morale here – but it could have been knocked'; another said: 'in another school it might have been very different'; and a third explained: 'It's the word "inspection", "HMI" - the whole impression you get. In fact it has given us a bit of a boost, but it could really destroy teachers if it had been a bad report.'

The same idea was expressed in two other cases. In one, a teacher said: 'we did OK, but it could drag you down'; and in another: 'what if there had been criticisms?' Two headteachers took this fear of failure a little further: 'what happens to the findings of other schools? Everyone knew that a local school had had a poor review'; and: 'I've heard of other headteachers being eased out.'

This brings back the question of accountability. There were just a few references to action which had followed inspections, negative consequences involving the loss of jobs. They were comments about other schools and, as such, part of the mythology, although they did offer some support to the idea that external action can follow external evaluation: 'It does have teeth. One of our county reviews was followed by an HMI inspection which led to the head's resignation. The head was anti the National Curriculum.'

During the course of the research a new mythology was emerging: the mythology of Ofsted inspection. One headteacher became very animated as he asserted: 'I've no time for this negative inspection that's coming. We're used to it being a two-way process. If you don't see your role as developmental and supportive, you'd better be sure that you are reporting fact, or you may have to justify it in court.' This was echoed by several inspectors:

'I'd see the Ofsted model as having more negative connotations.'

'Ofsted is becoming a kind of mythology – a bit like primary-secondary transfer.'

'I'm yet to be convinced by the Ofsted approach – people are running ragged to paper over the cracks. It has to be more than an accountability exercise; we are constantly hitting teachers over the head.'

We can see the judgement–development tension running through these comments, with undertones of the potential negative consequences of accountability, particularly now that 'failure' in an Ofsted inspection can be followed by 'special measures'. It has been difficult to find glimpses of light to brighten the inspection myth. The overall pattern of expectation set up by teachers, headteachers and inspectors had a significant emotional element. As teachers and headteachers have tried to make sense of inspection, the fear of failure has dominated. Their intense personal identification in what was intended to be an institutional event has dwelt heavily on the negative – monstrous – potential of inspection. The comments of the inspectors, far from offering a more positive and optimistic picture, have served more often to intensify the darkness. The ritualistic aspects of the inspection process have added to the sense that the individual inspection is subject to larger forces. The expectations and preconceptions of the participants in these case studies seem to suggest that judgement may defeat development.

3 GATHERING EVIDENCE

In this chapter I shall explore the procedural pattern of inspections and problems associated with inconsistencies in procedure. I shall look closely at the four main data-gathering methods used: examining documents, sampling children's work, interviewing, and classroom observation. The style and behaviour of inspectors in classrooms seems to be particularly significant to their credibility.

Despite the fact that Wilcox (1992) argued that inspection lacks an agreed methodological base, and Dean (1982) suggested that the procedural rules are unclear, the 12 inspections studied had a fairly consistent procedural pattern (see Table 3.1). This pattern is now enshrined in the Ofsted framework.

At the core of every case has been the making of judgements. With one exception these judgements were based on evidence which had been systematically gathered. In this exceptional case, the inspectors appear to have decided within hours of their arrival at the school that there was no cause for concern and switched their emphasis to giving developmental advice. Some of the teachers thought that they were still being inspected and were, understandably, critical of the procedural inconsistencies which then followed. However, the consistency with which inspectors have gone about their task has, in every case, been a common preoccupation for both the inspectors and those inspected.

Table 3.1

					Case studies								
	1	*2*	*3*	*4*	*5*	*6*	*7*	*8*	*9*	*10*	*11*	*12*	*Total*
Lead inspector briefs the head and asks for extensive documentation	yes	no	yes	yes	yes	yes	yes	yes	yes	yes	yes	yes	11
Lead inspector briefs the staff	yes	no	no	yes	yes	yes	no	yes	yes	yes	no	yes	8
Inspection team meet together before the visit	no	no	yes	yes	no	yes	yes	no	no	no	yes	no	6
Inspection team is introduced to the staff on arrival	no	yes	no	yes	no	no	no	no	yes	yes	no	no	4
Inspectors gather evidence through:													
• classroom observation	yes	yes	yes	yes	yes	yes	yes	yes	yes	yes	yes	yes	12
• work-sampling	no	no	no	yes	yes	no	no	yes	yes	yes	yes	yes	7
• interviews with teachers	yes	no	yes	yes	yes	no	yes	yes	yes	yes	yes	yes	10
Inspectors feed back to subject coordinators	no	no	no	no	yes	no	no	no	no	yes	yes	yes	4
Inspectors feed back to headteacher	yes	yes	yes	yes	yes	yes	yes	yes	yes	yes	yes	yes	12
Inspectors feed back to staff	yes	yes	yes	yes	no	yes	no	yes	no	yes	no	yes	8
Inspectors feed back to governors	no	no	no	yes	yes	yes	no	yes	yes	yes	yes	yes	8
Inspectors write a report	yes	no	yes	yes	yes	yes	yes	yes	yes	yes	yes	yes	11

The notice given to the school for its inspection ranged from 4 to 28 weeks.

Procedural consistency

Procedures could break down before the inspection had really got started. In two cases, the lead inspector changed the dates for pre-inspection visits, causing some initial irritation. In one of these two cases, the situation was compounded by a change in the inspection team just two days before the visit was due to begin. The school had been asked to arrange the timetabling of the inspectors' classroom visits. The change in personnel apparently necessitated substantial adjustments to this timetabling. Understandably, this was a cause of some resentment.

It is difficult to assess the significance of procedural breakdowns and inconsistencies. In the case just cited, there was a succession of procedural difficulties: interviews were conducted in different ways; some inspectors gave individual feedback to teachers while others did not; the inspectors' conduct in the classroom ranged from 'sensitive' to 'rude'; the inspectors did not keep to the expected timetable; and teachers were unclear about the requirements for the work-sampling. Nevertheless, the headteacher felt that she 'recognised the school' in the inspection report and 'agreed with all of their findings'. There were teachers in the school, however, who felt very differently, particularly those who were most implicated in the issues raised. They were not inclined to accept the key finding about low expectations. They were able to use the procedural confusion – 'it was a ramshackle affair; they had not got their act together' – to dismiss the validity and reliability of the inspectors' findings.

In contrast, another case was a model of procedural consistency: 'They told us exactly what they were going to do and did it.' Here, everyone within the school was agreed that the way in which the inspection had been carried out had been one of the major factors in its 'success'.

We begin to be faced with the question: 'What makes a successful inspection?' For those who see an inspection as providing an accurate judgemental picture of the school, the procedures for gathering the necessary evidence to paint a comprehensive representation are crucial. For those who may be looking for a more developmental outcome from an inspection, the issues surrounding the inspectors' interpretation of evidence move into sharper focus, as do the different ways in which findings are shared in oral feedback.

For the inspectors, there was often a procedural preoccupation with 'doing the job properly'. This reflected the prevailing sense that inspection was an important experience in the teachers' professional lives. The way in which the inspection was carried out was contributing to their professional code.

Procedural consistency seems to have been viewed in three different ways:

- did the inspectors do things in the way they said they were going to?
- did each inspector in the team do things in the same way as the others in the team?
- did the inspectors do things in the way that the teachers expected and in accordance with their sense of fairness?

In four cases, there was no pre-inspection briefing of the staff by inspectors. In all four of these cases, this caused significant misunderstandings. In two of these, there was extensive written procedural detail available. One was supported by a full set of LEA procedures; the other was being conducted in accordance with the Ofsted handbook. The misunderstandings seemed to revolve around the way in which the headteacher viewed the inspection. In the case where there was a full set of LEA written procedures, the lead inspector assumed that the headteacher would brief his staff. It appears that he did so, but without reference to the LEA's procedures. The lead inspector suspected that he might have been trying to undermine the credibility of the inspection. In the case conducted in accordance with the Ofsted handbook, the headteacher took the view that her staff would have been made more anxious if addressed by the lead inspector. She was trying to play the inspection down in their minds and decided to tell them very little, perhaps not realising herself the complexity of what was to come.

In one of these four cases, the headteacher was probably most successful in taking control of the inspection as a whole. The inspectors had sought permission to carry out the inspection partly as an opportunity for them to practise their skills. The headteacher was protective of teachers who had had a 'bad experience' during a previous inspection. The lead inspector felt that the headteacher had 'acted as gatekeeper'. When the inspectors arrived, they found that they had been programmed to visit certain classes and that the school's timetable had been reorganised on their account. There was a mismatch between what the inspectors wanted to do and what the school had prepared for them.

In the fourth of these cases, the headteacher was briefed by a different inspector from the one who subsequently led the team. Since, anyway, the inspectors changed their emphasis during this inspection, a direct meeting between lead inspector and staff beforehand might only have made matters worse.

Where the lead inspector did meet with the staff beforehand, there were considerable differences in the degree of detail offered about what was going to take place. One case stood out. The lead inspector rehearsed the inspection in considerable detail. He had already briefed the head who had, in turn, briefed the staff, so the teachers in this school had twice been told exactly what to expect. Following this, the inspectors kept consistently to their brief. Although the teachers at this school had rather vague notions about what the purposes of inspection might be, all except one viewed the inspection very positively and cited the consistency with which it had been carried out as a key factor. Their only complaint was that the inspectors had spoken directly to parents, which they had not expected. The one teacher who viewed the inspection less positively did so for quite different reasons – he felt most threatened in the face of judgements over teaching quality.

Not every lead inspector was as successful in briefing the staff. This was mainly related to the all-important human dimension of establishing relationships between inspectors and inspected which I shall explore in detail later. Otherwise the problems lay more in the different ways in which members of the team carried out the inspection than in what was or was not said at the pre-briefing. There was one particular aspect of procedure where teachers' expectations were not met: the giving of feedback. As one teacher said: 'The biggest mistake of the inspection to my mind was not giving everyone the chance to be debriefed after the lesson. I don't care how much it costs – if you write a report on someone, then dialogue with them is essential – it should be a common courtesy. For ten minutes even, that would be better than nothing.'

The importance of this strong statement is that many teachers expected individual feedback. I shall explore why this might have been at a later stage; at this point the issue is the mismatch between what teachers expected and what inspectors actually did. If the lead inspector had clarified expectations over feedback in the pre-briefing, there were at least four instances where the message had not been received by the teachers. Subsequently, the problem was compounded by the subtly different ways in which inspectors communicated messages to teachers about what they had seen and by the particular difficulty presented when an inspector had not approved of what had been observed.

The issue of whether feedback should be given and, if so, how, has probably been the main mismatch between what teachers have expected or been led to expect and what has actually happened. This mismatch is likely to continue. Ofsted is advocating that inspectors should engage in 'professional dialogue' with teachers whenever possible. I shall say more about this in Chapter 6.

Another confused aspect of inspection procedure has been the start of the inspection visit itself. In only four cases did the inspectors meet formally as a team with the staff on arrival. In view of the frequency with which the inspectors themselves have referred to the importance of establishing relationships with the staff, this might be seen as surprising. However, one inspector described how difficult it was to find anything useful to say when all the staff were lined up to meet all of the inspectors in the staffroom before school on the first day. HMI seem to have an arrangement by which inspectors can arrive at any time during the first morning of the inspection visit. In the two cases where HMI were involved they came to the school separately and the teachers met the team one by one as they appeared in their classrooms. In the other cases where the team did not meet together with the staff, there seems to have been tacit agreement that they should enter the school together. Several inspectors refer to their having waited in the car park for colleagues to gather; in one case the teachers described how they watched this happening. One headteacher described how the team 'marched into the school in single file with their briefcases'. There seemed to be a ritualistic element to this. In a different case, one of the inspectors said the start of the inspection 'felt like a group of people turning up for a course'.

In some schools, the start of the inspection took teachers by surprise: 'We'd been told they would not come to the classrooms straight away – I had an inspector in my class while I was still taking the register!' In this inspection, the teachers were still trying to work out which inspector was which on the third day. This difficulty in identifying people was common to several inspections. The message which seems to have emerged is one of teachers liking to know what is going to happen when and being discomforted by the unexpected. Since many of them felt that their personal performance as teachers was on the line, this is unsurprising.

The inspectors' concern to 'get it right' manifested itself in different ways, according to their perception of what they were trying to do well. Some inspectors were preoccupied with the human aspects of the inspection and were concerned, in everything they did, to recognise how the teachers might have been feeling. Some inspectors were more preoccupied with the volume of evidence they needed to gather and, on occasions, neglected the niceties of protocol. Some inspectors were particularly concerned to ensure that their views accorded with a team perception and focused on the ways in which a corporate view would emerge. There were contrasts between inspectors who were anxious to form an accurate judgemental view of the school, those who were looking to tease out and confirm the school's view of itself, and those who wanted to make a more direct contribution to the school's development.

In one inspection, the inspectors realised that they had not asked the teachers for their records. They apologised so profusely for asking the teachers to present their records at short notice that they drew attention to their mistake. Two teachers commented that they would not really have noticed the difficulty had it not been drawn to their attention. Nevertheless, the concern the inspectors had felt seemed to help to build a positive relationship between them and the staff.

A number of these smaller details of procedure appeared as isolated incidents in the overall pattern of the 12 cases. In one inspection, one of the inspectors wandered around the school, apparently losing herself several times. This was interpreted by two teachers as a deliberate strategy. They saw it as giving the inspector the opportunity to pick up on a range of evidence without appearing to do so. The inspector's view of it was that she had difficulty finding her way about, commenting that a map would have been useful. In another case, two teachers commented that the inspectors' contrasting styles had been deliberate – one rather distant and formal, the other sensitive and friendly. The impression the teachers gave was akin to the stereotype of two detectives questioning a suspect. In both of these examples, we can see how the teachers were attempting to make sense of what was going on by projecting their own interpretation on to the inspectors' behaviour.

Another procedural detail related to how different members of the team might work together. In the inspection where the pre-briefing was particularly thorough, the lead inspector told the staff that the inspectors would be seen talking to one another. He explained that teachers should not be alarmed. The inspectors would be comparing notes on what they had seen to try to arrive at an agreed view. In this inspection, teachers were also told that inspectors would only visit classrooms singly. Both of these points caused concern in other inspections. In one, three teachers referred to their anxiety about what inspectors might be saying to one another as 'they stood around whispering in pairs'. In two other cases, teachers described how threatening it was when there were two inspectors in the classroom together.

The core procedures of the cases related to the four different ways in which evidence was gathered: through documentation, work-sampling, interview and classroom observation.

Evidence-gathering procedures

Documentation

Several inspectors emphasised the importance of the documentation provided by the school although this was not a universal view. One inspector said that she did not bother much with reading documents in advance as she wanted to form her own view of the school. Another inspector felt that she had found out enough about the school from the team briefing. Generally though, inspectors felt that 'a careful analysis of documentation is essential'. 'It gives you indicators of what to look for.' 'Documentation gives me a way in beforehand – I can raise questions, but not too firm a hypothesis.' 'By reading, I don't waste time when I am there.' Despite some probing, it was difficult to find any particular pattern or approach in inspectors' analyses of documentation. In the earlier case studies, the insights gained into the school appeared to be more general than specific, random rather than focused. In the later case studies, which were often closely related to Ofsted procedures, there was a stronger sense of the documents being looked at against criteria, with questions being raised to guide the data-gathering during the inspection visit. In one of these later cases, two inspectors felt that they had been given a false impression of the school by the documentation; it suggested better practice than they subsequently observed. The Ofsted procedures themselves suggest that inspectors should be forming initial 'hypotheses' about the school from the documentation.

The schools' perception of providing documentation for the inspectors sometimes seemed to miss the connection between policy and practice. Several of the schools which were inspected after the advent of the Ofsted handbook seemed to see documentation as an end in itself as if they were satisfying a separate statutory requirement. In one school, a full set of documents was written and put together after the inspection had been notified. They were immaculately presented in spiral bindings, making it very difficult for the inspectors to photocopy them for analysis. In another school, the only existing documents were topic planning sheets. A series of policies and guidelines was hastily put together. There was some resentment when it appeared that the inspectors had not looked at the original planning sheets. More generally, however, even if some teachers and headteachers appeared not to have quite understood the place of documentation within the school's management systems, there was a widespread acknowledgement that the inspectors had read them. There were repeated comments about how 'they had done their homework', with some surprise expressed about how much the inspectors seemed to have found out about the school before they actually arrived. Despite the varied practice of the inspectors, and the different value they placed on documentation, there was only one case where there was speculation as to whether an inspector had read the paperwork the school had provided.

Work-sampling

In seven cases, the inspectors asked the staff to gather samples of work together for a formal work-sampling. Again, there seemed to be some variation in the seriousness with which this data-gathering approach was taken by inspectors. From the teachers' point of view, it seemed to generate considerable anxiety. They were worried about which children to select, about the presentation of the work, whether it had been consistently marked, and whether they could provide sufficient material to cover all of the subjects. More fundamentally, they were probably acutely aware that what they presented for the work-sampling reflected the quality of their own teaching.

In keeping with other aspects of the ways inspectors worked as a team, most teachers seemed relatively unaware of what might have happened during the work-sampling. They did not seem to have experienced this approach to evaluation themselves, except in one school where a preparatory work-sampling was carried out. Here, one of the teachers recognised its potential significance. She pointed out that inspectors could look for 'standards, differentiation, progression, continuity and the richness of the learning experiences enjoyed by the children'. Another teacher suggested that 'once the work-sampling had been done, the inspectors knew all they needed to know about the school'. In reality however, the work-sampling does not seem to have been as significant to the inspectors' judgements as some teachers might have expected. This may be in keeping with Winkley's (1985) observation that inspectors, particularly those with an LEA advisory background, are not used to working together. However, even HMI did not seem to have a clear procedure for work-sampling. In one of their inspections, the work-sampling was a cursory, rather superficial, affair, used primarily to reinforce judgements based on classroom observation. Only one inspector looked for progression in detail and little attempt was made to compare notes with colleagues. In a separate case, an HMI, while claiming that the work-sampling was a 'useful exercise', confirmed that 'there is much we could do to make our work-sampling more systematic'.

One team had had some training in work-sampling. They considered it to be an important part of the inspection. An inspector in this team cited how several of the main findings of the inspection were based on the evidence of the work-sampling. This view was supported in another case where the inspector felt that the evidence of the work-sampling was 'more secure because we could look at it together and agree our judgements'. In general, however, inspectors admitted that they had not had sufficient experience of formal inspection to have come to grips with forming judgements from work-sampling. Indeed, there were some inspectors who admitted that they lacked experience in any systematic gathering of evidence. This would fit with Becher Eraut and Knight's (1981) suggestion that inspectors' work in school is frequently described as 'superficial and impressionistic'.

The gathering of evidence through documentation and work-sampling takes place at one remove from a face-to-face interaction. In these approaches, teachers had little perception of procedural inconsistency even though there has been widespread suggestion from inspectors that neither approach has been as systematic or consistent as it might be. By contrast, in interviews and classroom observation, teachers and inspectors could see each other at work. As a result, teachers could look for and find technical weaknesses which would give them the chance to displace the validity of the inspectors' work. As Becher Eraut and Knight (1981: 78) point out: 'people find ways of rejecting the results of external evaluation'.

Interviewing

The significance of interviewing in the inspection varied from case to case. In two of the earlier cases, the inspectors offered interviews to the teachers as a chance to discuss their career. These discussions were less to do with inspectorial evidence-gathering and more to do with advisory work. If inspectors interviewed in the context of career development, we have an explanation for why teachers interpreted inspection as significant to their personal careers. This was particularly true where the inspectors gave the teachers clear indications of the quality of their classroom performance, based on the evidence gathered for an inspection report in which they would not be individually recognised. The teachers valued these interviews. They appreciated the personal feedback and the interest of the inspector-adviser in their professional progress.

In the other eight cases where interviews took place, the interviews were part of the evidence-gathering procedure. In one case, the LEA had only recently included interviews as part of the standard procedure. The lead inspector was nervous about how the teachers would take to the innovation. In the event, most of the teachers valued the opportunity to meet with the inspectors face to face. There was a standard set of questions which, except with one inspector, the teachers found they could answer without feeling 'interrogated'. There was confusion and disquiet over the inclusion of a set question about equal opportunities. Several teachers speculated that this was a particular bee in the bonnet of one member of the team. In fact, the question was part of the LEA procedures. It is possible, however, that this speculation was fed by the different interviewing style adopted by this particular inspector. One teacher described it as 'a grilling, very aggressive – it made me defensive. Other staff felt the same way – fractious rapport. Her approach in the classroom was the same – there was always a "but". It was a strong contrast to the rest of the team – she had a real presentation problem. She was doing what she was there for. The interview could have been developmental but it wasn't – it was a lost opportunity – she was a very knowledgeable lady.'

Two issues emerge from this description: the interpersonal style of the inspector; and the expectation of developmental feedback. In the cases more closely related to the Ofsted framework the practice emerged of teachers being interviewed twice in their role as subject-consultants. This provided an opportunity for inspectors to gather information during the first interview and then to provide feedback during the second interview. The inspectors had prepared questions for the first interview and had shared them with the teachers. As a result, the teachers seemed to know what to expect, although their perceptions of the experience varied.

There was an initial expectation that the interview would be a cross-examination. For some, that is exactly how it was experienced – 'an interrogation', one teacher called it – whilst for others, it became a 'discussion'. This difference of perception seemed to have originated sometimes in the style of the inspector, and sometimes in the level of the teacher's confidence. Teachers with less confidence seem to have found the experience of interview to be more harrowing. One inspector described how she attempted to put teachers at their ease but suggested that there had been occasions when her attempts had only served to make matters worse.

The experience of the second interview in the Ofsted-related cases also varied. Some inspectors went much further than others to provide suggestions to help the teacher to address the issues being raised. The teachers certainly appreciated this kind of interview more than those where they were just given the findings of the inspection. One inspector pointed out that there was insufficient time to discuss suggestions and that 'besides, it is for the school to decide how it wants to do things'. In one situation a paradox emerged. When the inspector made it clear that the meeting was just for the giving of feedback, the teacher felt somewhat powerless, yet the inspector's intention was to empower the teacher by leaving her to solve the problems for herself. Perhaps the teacher would have been able to do this if she had felt more ownership of the problems she was being told she would have to solve.

One teacher suggested that the inspectors did not need to observe in classrooms as they would have found out all that they needed to know from their interviews with subject coordinators. In the context of the inspection to which she was referring, there may have been some truth in this. It was not typical of most other cases because the inspectors were more interested in fostering development in their subjects than in judging the standards of achievement in the school. There was a much greater emphasis on the inputs of curriculum management and teaching than on the outcomes of learning and achievement. Their agenda for the inspection seemed to be as much to negotiate a set of criteria about their subjects with the school as it was to gather evidence on what was taking place. The inspectors did form a view about the quality of their subjects within the school but were not successful in communicating it, particularly as their view did not match the school's view of itself. The interviews in this case were seen as constructive by both inspectors and teachers; they conformed closely with a well-established set of expectations concerning advisory development.

In two cases, teachers complained that their interviews with inspectors took place during their lunchtimes when they wanted to relax or prepare for the afternoon. They felt that this weakened their position for the classroom observation which was to follow, but, more especially, felt that the time constraint made a proper conversation difficult.

This complaint points to a central issue in the way several teachers have talked about their experience of being interviewed: power. Repeatedly, teachers have commented about the way that the inspector has called the tune. Except in the cases where the interviews have focused on career development, it has been the inspectors who have set the agenda. Several teachers have resented this. They have wanted to have the opportunity to ask questions; they have not been sufficiently clear about the overarching agendas of the inspectors themselves; and they have often felt that their perceptions and opinions have not been sought or valued. In an extreme case, a teacher reported that 'it would not have made much difference if the interview had never happened. I wasn't happy. He wasn't interested – he had a set spiel and didn't look me in the eye. I wanted to explain. It wasn't really an interview – it was a disaster.'

In this inspection, the interviews seem to have been overshadowed by the negative impression that the whole inspection team had formed about the school. The inspectors seem to have kept the interviews rather short. The teachers in this case reported that they sensed that there were 'hidden agendas' and that the inspectors were 'ill at ease'. Some of the teachers openly acknowledged that the school was in need of major development. They had wanted to engage in dialogue with the inspectors but had not been able to do so.

The opportunity to talk with an inspector, one to one, seems to have been a very important part of the inspection for many, if not most, of the teachers. They have described how carefully they prepared for their interviews and, in several situations, their sense of the interview's success or failure appears to have coloured their perception of the inspection as a whole. The inspectors do not seem to have accorded the same significance to the interviews, although several acknowledged that this was a key opportunity to develop relationships; some emphasised the importance of the interview in beginning to secure the school's acceptance of the inspection findings.

The interviews have also been important to the credibility of the inspectors themselves. Several teachers have commented on the sharpness of the questioning, using such adjectives as 'deep', 'acute', 'shrewd' and 'perceptive'. Moreover, there was evidence that teachers 'compare notes' over the performance of inspectors. Although they have not featured strongly in teachers' responses, the skills of the inspectors do seem to have played a part in creating a perception of the inspection as a 'professional' event and in determining the willingness of teachers and headteachers to accept what the inspectors have to say.

But it was in the way the inspectors undertook their classroom observation that the key to their credibility could be found. This has been where almost every inspector has placed the greatest emphasis, outlining in considerable detail the approach taken. It has also been the part of the inspection which seems to have impinged most directly on the teachers' consciousness.

Classroom observation

Although it was in the classroom that inspectors seemed to gain most credibility, or occasionally to lose it, the question of credibility had often been raised before the inspection visit began. In one case, all of the inspectors were subject specialists with a secondary background. As a result, the headteacher and most of the teachers seemed to have been hostile to the team before they had even arrived. One of the inspectors, in particular, managed to overcome this hostility by the way that he consistently interacted with the children, demonstrating that he could talk to them relaxedly and with humour. As this headteacher put it: 'Credibility is the big word. You want to know when they were last in school – in a classroom. Had they ever worked in a primary school?'

In another case, several teachers were also preoccupied by the fact that two of the team were going to be 'secondary' inspectors. As it turned out, this concern disappeared as the inspectors were able to show that they could conduct themselves appropriately in the classrooms: 'We were impressed with them all. They must be able to empathise – close to the shopfloor. The misgivings and mutterings about their primary experience were not borne out in practice.'

In general, phase credentials were an easy target when a teacher had not been impressed by the conduct of an inspector. There were repeated references such as 'the inspectors with a primary background got involved with the children' (implying that others did not); or 'she had no primary perspective'. These comments tended to be dismissive and non-specific. However, in one case the difficulty was clearer: 'She took a whole day getting used to children asking her questions. Her lack of first-school experience was a weakness. She asked one child a question and it completely destroyed the process.'

Those inspectors who had a secondary background were very aware of the difficulty. They expressed particular insecurity about inspecting subjects other than their own. This was a point picked up by one teacher who questioned the validity of the findings when 'a non-musician was doing [inspecting] the music'. But, in general, subject credentials were not the main issue for teachers. They appeared to be looking at how inspectors interacted with children. In fact, most of the inspectors had undertaken extensive work in primary schools since they had become inspectors. As one put it: 'I have won my primary spurs.' However, the inspectors' self-concept did not always match the teachers' perceptions. An inspector with a secondary background recounted that he used 'the criteria of long experience. I have the credibility of long service.' Yet the teachers found him 'intimidating and insensitive'; one teacher described him as 'sticking out like a sore thumb in the classroom'.

Credentials were not only related to phase background. There was also the question of the inspector's experience as an inspector. In one case, there was conflict between the headteacher and one of the team because this inspector 'went to work on the budget'. He had only just become an inspector. The head knew this and appeared to be trying to exploit it, but a colleague inspector did suggest that the way in which the budget issue had been pursued was 'somewhat overzealous'. Several inspectors commented about how insecure they felt when inspecting an aspect of the school that they had not previously encountered. This was more a matter of inspectorial experience than of phase experience.

When the inspectors described their classroom style, a range of preoccupations emerged. These are comments from three different inspectors in the same case study:

'I try not to interfere or to cross-question the teacher. I might need to ask a question. I try to talk to the children – sit down, walk around – I try to avoid the "corner clipboard mode" – I sometimes hear children read.'

'I like to keep as low a profile as I can, involved but not deflecting from what is going on, stepped back but observing – specific and general together. Being seen to be as much a part of the school as one can. Not on the same side as the teachers as such, but alert, giving the teachers a good opportunity. I tend to note keywords. I'm affected by the teaching style of the teacher.'

'Sometimes I had to sit and listen. It gets easier as the inspection goes on. They become less anxious to perform. The pupils get to know you. Things shake down.'

More often than not, teachers did feel that the inspectors had managed to be 'unobtrusive'. Several inspectors seemed worried about how they made their entry into classrooms: 'I try to slide in, just making eye contact'. Some teachers seemed more interested in how the inspectors left the room than how they arrived. One inspector was described as 'downright rude. She came and went without a word.' But in general, teachers often mentioned that 'you could forget that the inspector was there', and that is how they seemed to like it. The contrast was with the conspicuously 'vertical' inspector who appeared in a few of the inspections. Some teachers complained that the inspectors 'insisted on asking questions when I wanted to get on and teach' and there was one case where a teacher recounted that an inspector 'unsettled me and the class – it was her body language – I think she was uncomfortable and that made me uncomfortable.'

The secret seemed to lie in how successfully inspectors mingled in with the children. If they did this, the teachers were happy, and the inspectors established credibility, overcoming many of the previous concerns there might have been with their credentials.

The requirements of Ofsted inspections include the completion of quite complicated lesson observation forms. Several inspectors were trying to find ways of doing this without being obtrusive. One teacher commented on how an inspector 'didn't talk to the children as much as I expected. He sat in the corner making copious notes. What is there to write about without talking to the children?'

For some teachers, the human anxiety of having an observer in the classroom seemed to obscure the main reason for the inspector to be there – to gather evidence. There was a strong sense that the experience of being inspected in the classroom had been rather harrowing. This did not necessarily relate to the teachers' competence – there were a few situations where inspectors alluded to poor practice but the teacher had not been threatened: 'We were doing a geography lesson which I thought was an absolute cracker. Subsequently they told us that geography was unsatisfactory. There was no discussion about why he obviously didn't like that lesson. I cannot see what was wrong with it. Different inspectors must be looking for different things.' Rather, it seemed to relate to teachers' confidence. In three different cases the headteachers reported that it had been their most accomplished teachers who seemed to have found the experience most draining.

But there were also many teachers who did appreciate what the inspectors were trying to do in their classrooms. There were frequent comments such as: 'They were here to observe; they knew what they were looking for and they found it'; and 'They have to have eyes in the back of their heads – they've got to not miss a trick.' In two cases, the lead inspector had gone into considerable detail at the pre-inspection briefing with the staff about what would happen in the classrooms and why the inspectors had to operate as they did. This seems to have made a difference. The teachers in these two cases had seemed more comfortable about what had taken place, even though inspectors had taken notes in the classroom. The only difficulty was that one inspector 'broke the rules by talking to us [teachers] more than she should have done'.

On just a few occasions, an inspector has conformed with the stereotype of a conspicuous presence in a classroom, brandishing a clipboard. In general, inspectors have studiously avoided this approach. I shall explore the extent to which inspection might distort what is being inspected in the classroom at a later stage. There is, however, the issue of whether the teachers' performance has affected the way in which the inspectors have behaved. Several inspectors have suggested that they have matched their style to the style of the classroom. 'If the teacher is talking to the whole class from the front, what can I do but sit quietly, listen, and observe?' Teachers have repeatedly alluded to the clipboard stereotype and it will no doubt persist in inspection mythology, even though very few teachers in the cases I researched had experienced this stereotype at first hand. Most teachers seem to have recognised what the inspectors were trying to do; have accepted that inspectors need to take notes; and have not complained when their own practice has made it impossible for the inspectors to talk to the children. Where they have complained is when the inspector could have talked to children but didn't or when the inspector seemed to talk to children somehow inappropriately.

The two face-to-face evidence-gathering situations – interviews and classroom observation – seem to have formed the core of teachers' perceptions of inspection. During the course of the research interviews, they often seemed to be structuring their idea of inspection in opposition to a notion of how they had thought it would be, a notion which seemed to be heavily dependent on the hearsay of myth. There has been a mixture of admiration and criticism.

The admiration has been for the way in which inspectors have often formed an acceptably accurate picture of the school so quickly; the criticism has usually related either to interpersonal discomfort or to the inconsistency with which one inspector has worked in relation to others. For some teachers, the criticism has reached the point where they have begun to question the validity of the inspectors' findings. In these cases, there has been an underlying resistance to the idea of being held accountable to a judgemental assessment of their practice – the teachers have been looking for ways to displace the findings. More generally, even when teachers have been able to pick holes in the inspectors' work, there has been an overall acceptance of the inspectors' findings as 'fair'.

Although the process of inspection has probably been more important to teachers than the outcomes as represented by the report and formal oral feedback, these outcomes have nevertheless featured strongly in the research interviews. For the headteachers especially, who did not personally experience classroom observation and were not always interviewed by inspectors during the inspection, the report and feedback have been the more important. In this context, further questions have been asked of the process. In particular, how did the inspectors reach this conclusion from the evidence that the teachers and headteachers thought they would have been able to gather?

4 ROLES AND

RELIABILITY

This chapter continues the discussion of the technical processes of inspection by looking at issues relating to the reliability of inspection judgements. It looks at the inspection team and at the key roles played by the lead inspector and the headteacher. This is followed by an exploration of the extent to which the turbulence caused by the inspection might serve to distort the validity of the inspectors' findings.

Evidence, criteria, judgement and the team

As the research for this book progressed, inspectors became progressively more preoccupied with evidence. In the cases undertaken using the procedures laid down by the Ofsted framework the inspectors had to complete a 'record of evidence'. These inspectors were particularly anxious that their judgements were sufficiently underpinned by evidence. One inspector described the 'job' of inspection as being 'to gather enough evidence to make judgements' and another maintained that 'being able to make judgements based on secure evidence' was the 'key factor in a successful inspection'. One of the headteachers concluded after the inspection that she would 'encourage the staff to keep more evidence'.

In the earlier cases, the significance of evidence seemed to have been appreciated best by those inspection teams who had the more carefully worked out standard procedures. In one of the LEA programmed reviews, an inspector described how she was 'every minute checking out' against evidence, that her 'observation methodology needed to be at its sharpest' and that the whole team took time to 'thrash out the findings, testing all the time against the evidence we had'.

However, in several of the pre-Ofsted cases, the search for evidence appears to have been more haphazard. The most extreme case was where a summative judgement about the school had been made within hours and the team moved into an advisory mode. In another of the earlier cases, it was apparent in the research interviews that the inspectors had formed strong opinions about the quality of what they had seen. These judgements were not, however, recorded in the report and they were not backed by detailed evidence. The inspectors appeared to have been working at a more general level, forming a view of the school more by intuition than by detection, relying on the 'connoisseurship' which has been described in much of the writing about how HMIs work (for example, Lawton and Gordon 1987).

The cases researched in this project seem to have charted a progression in the process of evidence-gathering, perhaps sharpened by the developing pressure of accountability in the culture of inspection.

In those inspections which followed the Ofsted framework, the evidence-gathering process was described by one inspector as starting with a 'scanning', whereby 'impressionistic evidence is assembled into an emerging view'. He suggested that thereafter the inspectors were 'looking for evidence which will either support or alter the judgements which are probably formed quite early on', but conceded that 'your view of the school can change. I have been in situations where I have had to revise my view of the school quite substantially on the last day.'

Another inspector described how the gradings from lesson observations are brought together to form a 'triangulated view' so that 'a corporate view' emerges. In a separate case, an inspector maintained that 'there could never be a statement [in the report] that we did not all agree with' and that, in the absence of sufficient evidence, 'things could therefore be left out'. He talked of the findings being 'thrashed out orally', a process which Wilcox (1992) describes as the time-constrained equivalent of analysing with a card index.

Although it may be possible to identify a core process by which a team arrived at corporate findings which were consistent with systematically gathered evidence, there has been considerable variation in the perceptions and understandings of both inspectors and teachers of any such process. Some inspectors have emphasised the need to be 'comprehensive' in their picture of the school whilst several teachers have suggested that this might lead to superficiality. One teacher commented: 'they missed the wider implications of things – they tried to be too comprehensive'; whilst another commented that 'they moved on too quickly'.

In the earlier inspections, and still persisting among some inspectors in the later cases, there was an emphasis on the 'impressionistic', connoisseurship approach: 'We are trying to find a shape as well as see'; we were 'looking for whole-school patterns'; and 'We were trying to unearth whether the school's view of itself was correct.' Within the same teams, other inspectors were talking of their difficulties in finding sufficient evidence, that a 'snapshot can give a misleading view'. Perhaps one teacher caught the tension between a precise, technical, evidence-based approach and a more impressionistic, intuitive and interpretative approach when she pointed out that the value of having a team of inspectors, as opposed to a singleton, is that 'the whole is greater than the sum of its parts'.

Teachers appeared to be more conscious of the judgements that inspectors made than of the evidence-gathering that preceded them. In several of the inspections, the teachers' preoccupation seemed to be more with the balance between judgement and suggestions or advice than it was between judgement and evidence. However, there were plenty of situations where the inspectors were criticised on the grounds of insufficient or unrepresentative evidence. A comment such as 'they didn't see enough to make a judgement' was typical of this kind of displacement attempt. One teacher pointed out with some animosity: 'A fill-in lesson was evaluated seriously as a maths lesson. It may have been a snapshot [inspection] but it wasn't a reliable piece of evidence to conclude on maths teaching.'

What we do not know is whether the inspectors did conclude anything from that one lesson, but it does reveal a difficulty for inspectors in establishing credibility for their findings. Similarly, a teacher suggested that an inspector had been 'bullshitted' (misled) during an interview with a subject coordinator with the result that the report did not represent an accurate picture. Certainly, there does appear to have been a loophole, even in the Ofsted procedures, whereby specific subject-related judgements could be reported without the same corporate scrutiny which had been directed to the overall findings about the school.

On occasion, teachers have expressed surprise or disappointment that some evidence has contributed to reported judgement. In one case, the teachers felt that the inspectors had missed deficiencies in their planning; in another that the quality of reading provision could not have been as good as the inspectors maintained; and in a third that it was 'galling that we didn't get credit for some of the specific things we do well'.

There are two further aspects of the evidence-gathering process which have raised questions about the reliability and credibility of the inspectors' findings: criteria and time.

Criteria

Until the advent of the Ofsted framework, writings about the work of inspectors, particularly HMI, have often referred to a lack of explicit criteria for inspection and have sought to discover the grounds on which judgements have been made. In general, this was not a preoccupation of those whom I interviewed although the issue of what the inspectors might have been looking for did emerge occasionally.

In the first case study, which examined an inspection which took place well before the Ofsted framework had come into being, the headteacher referred to the difficulty of 'global grapeshot'. There was a suggestion that the inspectors could make up the rules as they went along, thus exacerbating a sense of the teacher as victim. In another of the earlier cases, the inspectors seemed to have been using the inspection to sharpen their own criteria and to negotiate them into the school. The main substance of their report was a set of criteria which the school could use for future development. In this case, an inspector explained that 'they are what you see at that moment', suggesting that it was part of the process to evolve criteria as you went.

This might suggest the notion of 'grounded theory'. However, even before the publication of an explicit set of criteria in the Ofsted framework, inspectors have consistently used a set of criteria to organise their evidence. It may be true that the inspectors have had to make sense of practice as they have found it, that their procedures were not tight, and that their judgements have been necessarily qualitative. However, it would be misleading to assume that they had been inventing their organising concepts as they went along.

In another of the earlier case studies, an inspector suggested: 'We are still not sharp enough about criteria. We got sidetracked. This undermines our credibility.' Although this inspection did significantly alter course, the teachers' perception about the shift did not relate to the criteria as much as to the underlying purpose of the inspection. Although inspectors have frequently alluded to the importance of criteria in the case studies, the teachers have generally been happy not to have explicit criteria and seem to have accepted implicit criteria as part of the inspectors' expertise. In the case to which I have just referred, a teacher said, 'they have points they're looking for. If they don't understand they would ask.' In one post-Ofsted case, the teachers had not studied the framework in any detail. One of them was happy that 'they knew what they were after'. In those cases which were LEA programmed reviews, the written procedures did not spell out criteria beyond listing the headings for the report. This seemed to be sufficient to satisfy most teachers, one of whom particularly commented that it was 'significant that we knew the headings in advance'. Indeed, apart from the reference to global grapeshot, which was intended to displace the validity of what the inspectors were saying, there was only one complaint about criteria. This was where a teacher remarked that an inspector had a 'bee in her bonnet', a comment which was supported by a colleague who seemed to accept that there 'is always something which the inspectors seem to pick up as the preoccupation of the moment'.

Time

In the course of an inspection, the inspectors need to gather evidence at quite a pace. Wilcox (1992) described inspection as 'time-constrained evaluation'. Interestingly, although the limited amount of evidence which could be gathered in just a few days could easily have been used by teachers to displace findings which they found unpalatable, there was no such complaint in any but the cases where the inspection was very short. Two of the inspections researched lasted just two days. In the first of these, it was the inspectors who felt that 'the scale of the task was just too big – two days were not enough'. None of the teachers mentioned this. In the second, the teachers felt that it was not long enough and that the inspectors drew false conclusions from their limited evidence. 'They said two days was enough. The learning circle cannot be picked up in just two days.' The more general sentiment seemed to be summed up in this comment: 'How could they do it in such a short time? They must have been very astute.'

Perhaps the reason why teachers did not pick up on what might have been a vulnerability in the evidence-gathering process was because they would not have wanted to endure the intensity which the time constraint placed on them for a moment longer. Certainly, inspection has proved to be an emotional experience, an outcome which will be explored more fully later.

Ritual

One inspector commented that 'time constraints make for ritual'. This is an issue which relates closely to inspection mythology and to which I shall return when I explore relationships in inspection. From a procedural point of view, the whole pattern of inspection, which has been remarkably consistent from one case to another, has taken on a sense of ritual. Almost all of the inspections were backed by some kind of written procedure, not unlike a liturgical order of service; the Ofsted framework might appropriately be likened to an official *Book of Common Prayer*. The emphasis placed by schools on gathering documents before the inspection has seemed often to have been driven by a sense that this is what inspectors expect, rather than by any deeper grasp of the relationship between policy and practice.

This sense that there were certain behaviours which were appropriate to the conduct of inspections surfaced several times. Teachers seem to have expected inspectors to 'sit at the back of the classroom taking notes'. Inspectors themselves have admitted to being 'more formal' when they are inspecting and teachers have commented how inspectors they had met in an advisory capacity had surprised them by being 'more distant'. The work-sampling, in particular, seems sometimes to have been undertaken by inspectors because it has been expected of them, rather than as a significant source of important evidence. Inspectors have been described as 'going through the motions' even when interviewing and one inspector was not sure why he was expected to spend five or six hours going through documents before visiting the school. One inspector had felt, when he had been undergoing his Ofsted training, that 'the laborious way in which the headteacher was given feedback' was 'absurd'. He commented that 'HMI always do it like that.'

The procedural rituals seem originally to have had sensible reasons behind their existence, even if inspectors and teachers have sometimes been slow to recognise them. Other rituals, such as the seemingly automatic 'falling into line' which has occurred at the beginning of almost every inspection, the formality in relationships, and a certain uniformity of dress, appear to have been driven more by human responses to the difficulty of sitting in judgement.

Working as a team

Perhaps one explanation of the ritualistic aspect to inspection lies in the fact that none of the teams who undertook the 12 inspections researched had worked as a full team before. Several of the inspectors had worked together in other teams, but it seems to have been a given that a new team was formed for each separate inspection. It is unsurprising that some of the teams experienced considerable internal tension as they attempted to work together for the first time under tight time-constraints; they may have needed the choreography laid down to be able to function effectively together.

In the event, the inspectors have generally been able to work surprisingly well together. The process which has been described so far has contained numerous potential points of breakdown. The whole business could be likened to walking a tightrope, with several teachers looking for ways to encourage the inspectors to fall off. We have seen how, in one inspection in particular, there were inconsistencies between what the teachers had been led to believe in the pre-briefing and what actually took place. The inspectors' performance was described as 'ramshackle'; 'they hadn't got their act together'. Teachers seem to have expected that the inspectors would have prepared themselves to present a corporate approach: 'I hope they'd talked about their demeanour in classrooms.' In reality, this seems to have been left very much to chance. One inspector commented that he was 'not aware of colleagues' preferred data-gathering technique'.

The inspectors needed to work as a team to ensure that their findings were securely grounded in evidence. In one inspection the five inspectors involved were trying to find common ground between their subjects. In the event there were five different reports. It was just as well that they did not attempt to report on standards and so a secure evidence base was less important. Theirs was ultimately more of an advisory than an inspectorial event. They were able to find a common approach to reviewing and developing their subjects which the school could accept, albeit at an inconvenient point in the school's development cycle. In this 'inspection', the teachers seemed to have looked upon the different inspectors separately, taking what they could from each one's contribution, without much expectation that they would speak with one voice.

In most cases, the inspectors placed emphasis on working as a team, particularly when arriving at overall judgements, but the teachers did not seem aware of the workings of the inspectors as a team. Although they did sometimes refer to the inspectors collectively, and although inconsistencies between the methods of different inspectors were revealed, particularly in how much feedback was given, there was more of a sense that teachers looked on the inspectors as individuals. So many of the salient comments related to one-to-one transactions that inspection seemed to be seen as an accumulation

of these individual exchanges. This may have been because most significant transactions occurred in this way: individual teachers met with single
inspectors for interviews; the concerns of individual teachers as subject coordinators could often be attributed to one individual inspector in the report;
the pre-briefing tended to be given by the lead inspector alone; feedback
would also be given one-to-one; and the comment of one inspector after
leaving the classroom often provided the memorable point for the individual
teacher.

When asked directly, teachers almost always said that they would prefer
separate visits by individual inspectors to team inspection. It is likely that
this says as much about teachers' preference for advisory visits over inspection as it does for their perception of inspectors as individuals within a team.
The inspectors may have perceived themselves as a team, but they only sat
down together when they were away from the teachers. If they were not
introduced as a team at the start of the inspection, the teachers could only
view them as individuals. Ironically, in one inspection where the team was
not introduced, the teachers were still trying to distinguish one inspector
from another on the third day of the inspection and this may have served
to create more of a team impression. However, the teachers did find the
anonymity of the inspectors in this case very unsettling.

The lead inspector

In this same inspection, the teachers were pleased when they were able to
talk informally with the lead inspector at the end of the third day to establish some kind of individual rapport. Where the lead inspector has taken
a lead, it appears that this has made a significant difference to the cohesion of the inspection overall and has helped the teachers to focus on the
inspectors as a team. The identity of the lead inspector was not always clear
to the teachers. There were four cases where teachers had difficulty in saying who the lead inspector was. For one of these, the problem may have
been associated with an absence of those situations where the lead inspector
establishes her position: no report was presented; there was no pre-briefing of
the staff; and the inspection was notified to the head by a different member
of the team. Moreover, in the LEA context, one member of the team was
known to be senior to the inspector who was meant to be leading. This was
an issue in other teams – a point to which I shall return when I explore the
human dimensions of inspection in greater detail.

In two of the other inspections where teachers were uncertain of the
leadership, this was because the leadership was shared. In both of these, the
inspection was, from the inspectors' point of view, run in the school by
one person but the report was written and presented by another. During the
inspection itself, the teachers in one of these felt that there had not been a
leader; in the other, they attributed the leadership to the inspector they
knew to be senior within the LEA, although the team was actually led by
their locally attached inspector. This confusion was compounded by the fact

that the senior inspector then wrote the report. There was no suggestion that the confusion over leadership made any particular difference; the teachers seemed to view the inspectors as individuals working in the school at the same time.

In the fourth of these cases, most teachers were able to identify the lead inspector because their headteacher had told them who had notified him of the inspection. However, given that this was the inspection where the five inspectors presented separate reports, it is perhaps not surprising that there were two teachers who were not sure who the lead inspector had been.

In two cases, the differences that could be made by an active lead inspector stood out. In one of these, the staff had already been briefed by another inspector who then had to withdraw from the team through ill health. She had upset the staff at the pre-briefing, giving them a somewhat intimidating account of what was going to take place such that she had raised staff anxiety to a high level. In the light of this, the appearance of a new lead inspector, who then briefed the staff again from a more accommodating stance, appeared to have raised the profile of his team leadership considerably. This inspector saw it as a priority to manage the feelings of everyone who was involved. He conceded that the quality of relationships in an inspection might not be significant to the validity of the report, but maintained that he would 'still prefer to be engaged in a human process'. The potency of his leadership lay in two factors: he assiduously checked out how the head, staff and his colleagues were feeling and continually nurtured their confidence; and he shared considerable detail with the headteacher about how he, the head, might contribute to the success of the inspection.

This was also a significant factor in the second of these cases. The lead inspector briefed the head in great detail so that the staff received two briefings, one from the head and one from him. In this inspection though, it was the relationship between the lead inspector and the head which seems to have made a significant difference. Unusually, the lead inspector was also the local attached inspector for the school. He saw the inspection process as lasting for several months as he worked to prepare the school for the inspection and to hint at the issues which he suspected would be raised in the report. He paid great attention to detail and also briefed his team so that they knew exactly what was expected of them.

The investment of time before the inspection seems to have made a difference to the smooth running of this inspection. At the same time, other members of the inspection team threw some doubt over the accuracy of the findings. Whilst there was agreement that the evolution of the team's findings was undertaken corporately, there was a sense that inspectors whose perceptions of the school did not match those of the lead inspector felt 'thwarted' and found him 'overbearing'. I shall explore later the question of the extent to which inspection findings might have been 'tailored' to match what the school might have been ready to hear. In this case, there was a stronger suggestion that the lead inspector might have been 'overprotective' of the school.

Where teachers saw the role of the lead inspector positively or with significance in other cases, two features stood out. The lead inspector had gone out of his or her way to present a human face; or the lead inspector had been seen to sort out a situation where a team member had caused upset. In one such situation, the staff had met with the headteacher at the end of the day – an arrangement which had been suggested by the lead inspector – and all had reported that one particular inspector had been brusque and had put them on edge in the classroom. The headteacher had reported this back to the lead inspector who spoke to the inspector concerned. The teachers had subsequently seen a difference in this inspector's demeanour.

This example illustrates what has appeared to be the most important aspect of the lead inspector's role: to liaise with the headteacher. Unlike the teachers, the headteacher has had no difficulty in identifying the lead inspector, for it was with this person that all of the preliminary arrangements for the inspection were negotiated; with whom, in most cases, continual contact was made during the inspection; and who has been responsible for presenting the findings both orally and in the report. This core relationship seems to have worked well in almost every case, even where the lead inspector had to make comments which challenged the headteacher's leadership or management of the school. There were exceptions. In one case, the headteacher was irritated by what he saw as a change in the rules of the inspection when the inspector switched from a more judgemental inspectorial agenda to a developmental advisory one. Here, the difficulty seems to have been compounded by an idiosyncratic head having a low opinion of the lead inspector's professional credibility. In a second case, the headteacher had expected strong validation of the school's provision in the subjects being inspected and found himself confronted by unexpected demands on his school's development agenda. In a third, the headteacher appeared to feel vulnerable and generated tension by failing to accept the spirit of the LEA's review procedures. As the lead inspector put it: 'The headteacher's lack of preparation was making a statement.'

In all the other cases, the relationship between the headteacher and the lead inspector seems to have worked well because the headteacher was as keen as the lead inspector for it to do so. In one case, the headteacher was supportive of the lead inspector despite the fact that several of her teachers were strongly critical of both the way the inspection had been managed and of the lead inspector's personal style.

The headteacher's role

If the lead inspector had a responsibility for managing the conduct of the inspection team and, in some cases, for helping to manage the emotional impact of the inspection on the staff, it has been the headteacher's role to manage the school's response to the inspection. The headteacher appears often to have made a significant difference to the way that the inspection has worked as a process and may on occasion have also affected the reported findings.

The headteacher's interpretation of his or her role in an inspection seems to have been affected, as with the teachers, by his or her level of confidence about what the inspectors might find and how these findings might be dealt with. In two of the earlier cases, the leadership of the headteacher had been an explicit reason for the inspection. In both of these cases, the headteachers seem to have kept a low profile: 'I tried to keep out of the way'. At the opposite end of the scale, two headteachers, in particular, attempted, proactively, to manage the whole process. In one of these cases, the headteacher seems to have been partially successful. The inspectors felt that 'the school had been successful in holding us at a distance'. Nevertheless, one of the inspectors in this team felt that the 'head had no concept of what this visit was about'. There was a very strong sense of loyalty to the headteacher amongst the staff at this school and the impression they gave suggested that, although they still felt personally exposed, they wanted to perform for the headteacher.

When he also only circulated extracts of the report to his staff, the sense of the 'headteacher as gatekeeper' was further strengthened. This was an extreme case. It seems to have occurred through a combination of a particular headteacher's management style, a lack of cohesion and confidence in the inspection team, and the fact that this inspection was 'negotiated': the school was asked if they would accommodate the inspectors rather than informed that they were coming. Despite all of this, the inspectors' findings were not what the headteacher had wanted or expected to hear.

In the other of these cases, the inspection had also resulted from some negotiation. The school had been offered the opportunity to participate in a 'pilot' inspection using the Ofsted procedures. Again, the headteacher had seen this as an opportunity for his view of the school to be positively validated. However, as one of his staff put it, 'He thought that he'd be able to manage the inspection, but events overtook him.'

In this case, in contrast to the previous instance, the headteacher was confronted by a clear set of procedures which forced him into the position adopted by most headteachers – to 'massage morale' and 'act as a supporter'. Several headteachers commented that they 'felt isolated' by the inspection once it had started. The focus of the inspectors was on the teachers and in classrooms. One lead inspector explained that the 'headteacher needs to be given a role'; he had suggested a daily staff debriefing 'to ensure that morale was properly managed'.

Several headteachers had clearly had their work cut out for them in the run-up to the inspection. In addition to gathering, or in at least two cases, writing documents, there had been more than one 'crisis of confidence' amongst the staff. There had been a debate about whether 'we should be seen as we are' or whether the school should 'put on a show'. Most headteachers claimed to have opted for the former, trying to encourage the staff to feel confident about the way they usually operate, although several teachers admitted that a show had been put on. Some heads had played an important part in helping the staff to understand the detail of what the inspectors were going to do.

Under Ofsted procedures, the headteacher has an important input into the inspection beforehand. A commentary is invited about the school's recent history, and a description has to be written about the school's catchment. Headteachers have frequently referred to their concern to give the inspectors a context in which to place their 'snapshot' inspection. One headteacher felt that the inspectors had thrown back at him his emphasis on disadvantage in the catchment area, by commenting on low expectations in the school. Others felt that the inspectors had not given due credence to how far the school had developed in the recent past. Understandably, headteachers who have wanted to place the inspection in a developmental context have hoped that the inspection will report on what has happened as well as point out ways forward. They have usually received pointers for the future, but the inspection report has almost always failed to give a historical account of where the school has come from, focusing instead on what has existed at the time of the inspection.

The turbulence and distortion of inspection

The debate about whether the school should lay on a show or 'just try to be normal' raises questions about how far the process of inspection distorts what it sets out to inspect. Although there has been some evidence to support this, it has not been clear from my research to what extent the overall account of the school which has emerged has been unrepresentative or, worse, invalid.

If it is accepted that all schools and their teachers will try to give of their best during an inspection, then, presumably, the inspection report will give an account of what the school considers its best to be. Thus, inspection reports may be said to give a picture of schools as they are during inspections. Moreover, the process of inspection, when properly undertaken, involves matching together different sources of evidence. It is unlikely that a school would be able to outperform itself to any significant extent, particularly if, as one teacher put it, 'they would see right through us if we put on too much of a show'; and as an inspector commented, 'The children let on if things have been changed.'

The inspections researched seem to have caused turbulence and some distortion to normality in several ways:

- tidying up the visual environment of the school;
- more thorough and detailed preparation for lessons;
- tactical teaching to manage potentially disruptive children;
- making room to accommodate the inspection team;
- premature completion of policy documentation;
- specific preparation for interviews;
- alterations to the teaching timetable;
- alterations to normal teaching provision;
- particular responses to the perceived expectations of certain inspectors.

The tidying of the school has been universal and frequently compared to how one might prepare at home for visitors. One headteacher alluded to 'preparing for the mother-in-law' and a teacher explained that 'you hoover round but you don't redecorate'. Another teacher suggested that it was 'like preparing for a parents' evening'. Displays have been 'titivated', 'overhauled', or 'changed two weeks early', and one school bought a set of pictures to decorate the corridors and entrance lobby. There has been no suggestion from teachers that this tidying-up has had any longer-term significance; nor have any inspectors referred to display in this context – their reports have sometimes made positive references to the school's visual environment but have equally made comments suggesting that it, or its use, could be improved. This particular aspect seems have taken on some ritualistic characteristics, although we will never know whether inspectors, individually or collectively, would have seen the schools differently had tidying-up not occurred.

The presentational aspect of teachers' responses to inspection also surfaced in their preparation for lessons. One teacher related that 'People made sure their plans were beautifully written – they [the inspectors] were impressed by student-style lesson plans.' In the course of the research interviews, several teachers referred to 'making sure that everything was up together'; they took special care over their short-term planning and to prepare fully before discussing their subject coordinator responsibilities with inspectors. This did not stop inspection reports from criticising teachers' short-term planning or from their asking for 'clarification of the role of subject coordinators'.

One aspect of particular concern in two cases was the worry about how the children would behave while the inspectors were on site. No one has ventured any suggestion as to how the children might be kept any more under control than usual, although teachers from several case studies recounted how they had asked the children 'to be on their best behaviour for visitors'. There have however been suggestions that this might have been a factor in the 'safety teaching' and that some children 'began to be particularly difficult as they got more tired' in the latter stages of inspections.

In one inspection, the inspectors criticised the arrangements the school made for watching educational videos, reporting that 'The accommodation was cramped and pupils found it difficult to see the television screen.' This caused considerable resentment amongst the teachers, who pointed out that the television was in a corridor area because the usual room had been given to the inspectors to work in. However, this issue did not appear to undermine the teachers' overall confidence in the inspectors' findings. It is arguable that the inspectors should have recognised the problem they themselves were causing, but people seem to have seen it as a relatively minor issue. In other inspections too, the accommodation of the inspectors caused short-term inconvenience. In one case, the headteacher vacated his room to give the inspectors somewhere to base themselves. This may have contributed to the 'feeling of being a spare part' which this headteacher experienced, but did not seem otherwise to have been of lasting significance. In another case, the inspectors were based in the staffroom. They recognised that their presence there stifled the teachers' conversation. This particular base for the team was unusual in that inspectors seem generally to have gone out of their way not to go into the staffroom so as to 'give the teachers space'.

Although the writing of papers which would not otherwise have existed may be seen as a distortion of the school's normal provision, this might also be seen as a significant outcome of inspection for, once written, they will have continued in existence and may well have been validated by inspectors' comments on the practice to which they refer. Except in one case, it would not be possible, from the comments by teachers and inspectors, to conclude that the existence of these policies significantly altered the inspectors' perceptions of the school. In this case, the inspectors felt that the impression they had formed of the school from the paperwork was significantly better than the school they found when they observed. In two cases, inspectors felt that the school had misconceived the place of such documentation in the inspection process, suggesting that there had been few policies before the inspection was notified.

In the later cases, where the inspections were conducted in line with the Ofsted framework, the approach to inspection appears to have become more subject-focused. As a result, when inspectors have asked teachers for timetables, they have sometimes needed to come back to the headteacher to ask for more subject-specific detail. This has irritated a few teachers, generating mutterings about 'secondary' inspectors, as they had expected the inspectors to be able to sort out for themselves an interpretation of 'topic' as a designation for slots on their timetables. Teachers in two cases felt that the requirement, as they saw it, to teach subjects in a purer form than usual had changed their classroom practice for the worse during the inspection. A whole staff felt that the findings on English were unfair. They had been criticised for teaching English in a 'fragmented' way, yet they claimed that this was because they had been asked to. In another case, carried out under an LEA's procedures, the school itself had been asked to arrange timetables on behalf of the inspectors. This caused immense frustration as the inspection team was changed twice within the last two days before the inspection visit started.

This was one of only two cases where the inspectors did not plan their own itineraries. (In the other, the headteacher had decided to arrange where the inspectors should go and when.) Two inspectors, both with a strong primary phase background, expressed some discomfort at the way that the Ofsted procedures seemed to be driving them and the teachers towards a subject focus and away from a more integrated interpretation of the curriculum, although one of them felt comfortable that he personally could 'find my subjects in a topic-based approach'.

The teachers' sense of injustice when their English provision was criticised does indicate a more significant distortion caused by the inspection process. Again, a trend towards a subject-focused provision might also be described as an outcome of inspection; there have been teachers in three schools who have alluded to staff discussion subsequent to the inspection which looked as if it would lead to a more permanent subject focus in their curriculum planning. This touches on a developmental effect of inspection, by which schools may have been shaped by the expectations of the inspectors' procedures or criteria, in addition to any specific recommendations made in the report.

Although most teachers, and almost every headteacher, have accepted the overall findings of the inspectors in their oral and written reporting, there have been several comments made about the effect of the inspectors on classroom practice. A few teachers have insisted that they 'do not behave differently with inspectors around'. However, many have suggested that they wanted to perform at their best, or at least to make sure 'to my satisfaction that my nose was clean'. In doing this, several have recognised that their practice changed. One teacher knew that 'it was much more structured than usual – I could not run my integrated day. Nothing ever got finished. It made the classroom feel very chaotic.'

Some teachers felt that they 'tensed up' when certain inspectors came into the room. One described how 'the negative rapport' she felt with one inspector meant that 'I went back to kids much sooner [i.e. she oversupervised them] than I normally would. I know that happened to other staff, saying they almost fell apart.' Another felt that she had 'set fewer deadlines for the children when the inspectors were around'. This school was criticised for 'lack of pace'.

Researchers have written quite extensively about the effect of observers on the practice they seek to observe. In the research interviews, however, most of the comments relating to the inspector-as-observer have either been concerned with their human and emotional effect on the teacher-as-person or with the inspector's data-gathering style. There seems to have been an underlying acceptance of the observer, provided that, as I have related previously, the inspector maintains credibility by talking appropriately to children and by being unobtrusive. If teachers have not talked more of the disruption caused by a classroom observer then I must conclude that they have not been disconcerted by it. There may be a little more to this: it is possible that they have been upset but have accepted a certain inevitability in being inspected in this way. I shall return to this point when I explore teachers' passive presentation of themselves in the context of inspection.

Inspectors and headteachers from several inspections have mentioned how many of the teachers 'play safe' during an inspection, taking few risks and providing children with work which keeps them in order. In one case, the headteacher felt that a reference to 'worksheets' in the report would not have been there if 'the staff had only taught as they know they can'.

Although teachers have said several times that 'it would have been silly to do anything special', suggesting that it would be difficult to mislead inspectors, it seems that they did construct a performance. One teacher felt that she worked much better when she had an 'audience'. Some mentioned that they were trying to work out 'what the inspectors wanted' and to provide it. In an extreme case, a teacher admitted that she had taught a set of lessons which she had worked out with an advisory teacher before the inspection. Another teacher, whose practice was identifiably praised in the report, taught a whole series of lessons which his colleagues insisted were 'completely uncharacteristic'. The irony of this particular instance is that the teacher enjoyed his 'artificial' style and, perhaps also in response to the positive reinforcement he had from the inspectors, continued to teach in this way thereafter. Again, a short-term distortion seems to have become a permanent outcome.

In the four cases carried out in strict accordance with the procedures of the Ofsted framework, the teachers were asked to have their short-term planning available in the classroom for the inspectors to look at. One headteacher and two of the inspectors commented that this made a significant difference to the quality of the teaching, as 'some teachers had to think very carefully about their learning objectives'. Since one of the criteria for the quality of teaching in the Ofsted framework is that teachers should have clear objectives for their lessons, it became a self-fulfilling prophesy that their practice would be stronger if they had already been asked for those objectives to be on view. This is another example where the criteria and procedures for inspection may have led, of themselves, to developments in a school's practice.

Despite the fact that there is considerable evidence to suggest that aspects of the inspection not only disturbed but also distorted what might normally have been happening in the school, I would like to return to the prevalent sense expressed by the headteacher who said 'I recognised my staff in the feedback and the report.' The assertions made about changed practice generally relate to small-scale items of evidence, only five of which have appeared in the inspectors' reported findings: the television space; fragmented English; insufficient pace; worksheets; and an identifiable reference to good teaching which it appears had been staged. None of these have appeared in the main recommendations or key issues of the report; they appear not to have affected the overall findings of the inspection (although it is possible that three such instances together might have affected the overall tenor of the findings in one case).

The generation of policies, the emphasis on individual subjects and the identification of learning objectives in short-term planning may have had a more substantial effect on the inspectors' overall findings. It is very difficult to disentangle these, all of which appear in the published Ofsted framework, and claim that the inspectors will have recorded a distorted picture of the school's usual provision. They appear to be examples of where inspection might, of itself, have made a difference, not just in the short-term but also in a more permanent sense. This being so, the inspectors will have described not only what they saw but what continues to be there. This is different from phenomena which were only there when the inspectors were also there.

5   FEEDBACK

This chapter looks at the way that inspection findings are fed
back, orally and in writing. It reveals the negotiation which
seems to go on, perhaps sometimes to the extent of
compromising the objectivity of the findings.

Reporting

Oral feedback to teachers

Teachers have been irritated when they expected feedback and did not receive it. Where did this irritation come from? And where, if anywhere, does
feedback fit into the processes of inspection?

There has been no dispute about the need for or expectation of formal
feedback to the headteacher. Where confusion seems to have arisen is in the
extent of the feedback given to individual teachers. In the inspections carried
out before the advent of the Ofsted framework, there was no formal feedback
to subject coordinators. In one of these earlier cases, the inspectors offered
'career interviews' to the teachers. In another, they interviewed subject coordinators and then moved into an advisory mode at the same sitting. In
these two cases, and the six others undertaken using LEA review or 'at risk'
procedures, some feedback was given to class teachers about their practice,
but only by some inspectors in the team, and only to some teachers.

This inconsistency has several possible explanations. Firstly, the inspectors
working on these cases all had an advisory background. They would have spent

more of their time visiting schools alone to offer developmental advice than they would have done working in formal inspection teams. Although, certainly in two cases, the inspectors were told that they should not give informal feedback to teachers, at least one inspector did so in every case. The teachers too would have been used to advisory visits from inspectors where they would often have received some kind of debriefing. It was not surprising that they would have continued to expect it.

Secondly, there is an ethical principle, relating to democratic evaluation, where inspectors and teachers might be seen as working together to make judgements and to identify issues for future development. In the inspection where a report was never written, this appears to have been because the inspectors and teachers wanted to write it together as a 'negotiated report'. The project was never completed but it fitted in with a 'right of reply' principle which accords with the development of the school self-evaluation approach during the 1970s and early 1980s and which has had its impact on modifications to the Ofsted framework. Although inspectors have not given much impression that they have a deep understanding of evaluation methodology or of its ethical underpinnings, there does seem to have been a desire at some intuitive level to recognise the teacher's right to access their deliberations in some way. The underlying tension between judgemental inspection and the more developmental potential of inspection has been close to the surface in many of their responses. One inspector wanted to 'leave each teacher with something' and another said that 'we should have debriefed every teacher'.

There seems to have been a fine line between 'the normal courtesies', where inspectors have felt that they should leave a classroom with some kind of a thank-you, and giving a stronger impression of what the inspectors have actually found. This kind of feedback seems to have been more likely when the inspectors have liked what they have seen. Several teachers have reported on how the 'little comments made' by inspectors have boosted their confidence; none has talked of negative comments, although one related how the inspector made 'several useful suggestions'. Overall, the problem was summed up by one teacher who said: 'A lack of feedback increases anxiety – everyone assumes the negative.' Weaker teachers seem to have been left with little.

Teachers have had some difficulty handling their personal anonymity in the context of formal inspection. The inspections have reported on the school as a whole but there has been no escaping that the overall findings were distilled from a large number of individual performances. Teachers seem to have felt personally accountable in all of the inspections. This personalisation has often lain behind the desire for feedback. There have been several comments such as: 'The staff wanted individual feedback'; and 'I'd like to have had a personal meeting.'

The fact that the inspectors have seen an individual classroom observation as only part of an overall picture appears to have been an important reason why this individual debriefing has been withheld. One inspector explained: 'It can be dangerous to say too much during the inspection about what we are seeing. There could be a mismatch between what a teacher is told about one lesson and what we then say about the school as a whole. Besides, it is supposed to be a corporate perception. If one inspector gave individual feedback, another inspector might not agree with his view.'

A shortage of time has compounded the problem. One inspector succinctly rejected the idea of individual feedback: 'There's no time for it.' Another suggested that 'It interrupts the flow.' Although some inspectors had wanted to give individual feedback, and several did so in some form, there were others who advanced a contrary human argument: 'Teachers get upset by an instant debriefing' and 'Teachers may not be ready for immediate feedback.'

In the inspections carried out using the Ofsted framework, the inspectors met with subject coordinators to share their findings. The practice seems to have grown up because some individual HMI favour it. There seem to have been three main reasons behind this practice: to give detailed information to the person who is best placed to use it; to provide more detail than could be fed back to the headteacher or written in the report; to 'leak' aspects of the inspection's overall findings as part of a 'negotiation of ownership'. A fourth reason was advanced by some: to provide an opportunity to give subject coordinators some advice. Other inspectors strongly disagreed with this reason: 'we are not there to make suggestions', and also pointed out that there wasn't time to give advice to all the coordinators.

Inspectors seem to have wanted to 'prepare the school for messages they may be receiving'. The idea of 'leakage' has often featured in discussions with inspectors, although the inspectors from two teams seemed surprised by the notion when asked about it. Nevertheless, one of these inspectors saw the point and felt that it had been 'inevitable but not deliberate' that teachers would have begun to form a view of what the inspectors were going to say. In one case, the lead inspector saw the inspection as involving 'two or three months of interaction – issues have been raised and discussed in such a way that the school think they raised it themselves'. His team all shared this idea of 'planting seeds'. They did not debrief subject coordinators but did use the career interviews they offered as an opportunity to give individual feedback.

In the inspections following the Ofsted framework, the idea seemed to be that the subject coordinators would disclose to the headteacher what the inspectors had said to them, thus preparing him or her for the findings which would be fed back all at once at the formal oral debriefing. Thus a head could say, 'I knew what would be said from the coordinators.' What the inspectors seem to have been aiming for is the principle that, when the inspection report is ultimately published, the school should already be fully conversant with everything that it contains. Some inspectors seemed to have wanted to bring this 'no surprise' element back in time to the point when the headteacher is formally debriefed. One lead inspector saw it as part of his role 'to keep the headteacher informed of how it is going'. In one inspection, this seemed to have moved slightly out of control: separate inspectors were giving feedback to the headteacher during the week while other inspectors didn't know what was being said – the corporateness of the team became fragile.

An issue of protocol developed around the debriefing of coordinators in two of the cases. In both, the lead inspector appeared to have been worried that coordinators would receive information before the headteacher did, despite the fact that the inspectors wanted leakage to occur. There was a fudge. The inspectors were briefed to tell the coordinator that they were giving the feedback 'in confidence'. They did not all remember to do this. When these teachers met with the headteacher that evening, some immediately passed on what they had been told, whilst others thought that they should not do so. 'We were a bit confused whether we were meant to tell the head or not.' In another inspection this was resolved by the lead inspector asking his colleagues to pass on to the coordinators the issues raised but not the harder-edged judgements of standards and quality. This compromise seems to have facilitated a developmental approach with the coordinators whilst retaining a protocol of keeping the summative findings for the formal debriefing of the headteacher.

Oral feedback to headteachers

The practice of feeding back to the headteacher seems to have been consistent across all cases. The lead inspector has sat down with the headteacher, often with the deputy headteacher also present, and has talked through the inspection team's entire findings. This has sometimes taken as long as three hours. As one head reported: 'It was the most stressful two-and-a-half hours I've ever had in my life.'

There seems to have been as strong a sense of ritual about this last stage of the inspection visit as when the inspectors first arrived. Several inspectors acknowledged that they 'put on a smart suit' and one inspector also noticed that 'All of the staff had dressed up in their glad rags – clearly there was to be a celebration after we had gone.' One inspector suggested that part of the reason behind the long debriefing session was 'to justify the time we have spent'. He seemed sceptical of the value of the session, which he saw as 'bombarding the head', and again, 'rather like giving someone the cane', perhaps suggesting that the inspectors might be blinding the headteacher with their science. Certainly, one head said that 'there was insufficient time to take in the detail' of what was said.

Particularly under the constraints of the tight procedures of the Ofsted framework, the lead inspectors seem to have been very nervous before this final session with the headteacher. This may have been why they wanted to hide behind their formal dress. In their accounts of the process of inspection, a strong desire to do the job well has frequently surfaced. Since the final session with the headteacher might be seen to be the climax of the inspection, it would have been the point at which the professional performance of the lead inspector was most exposed.

One inspector, who had accompanied the lead inspector at the headteacher's debriefing, described how the session had been conducted: 'The lead inspector introduced the session, making it clear that the inspectors' findings could only be challenged for factual accuracy. There were several situations where the head wanted to discuss what was being said. The lead inspector was very strict – advisory discussion was out of order.' This seems to have been an inspection where the school was quite heavily criticised. It is possible to see from the way her colleague described the session how the lead inspector was protecting herself so that she could get her messages across.

Although recommendations have always been made at these sessions, presumably with a developmental intent, in the ebb and flow between judgemental and developmental standpoints, the debriefing of the headteacher seems to have been, in almost every case, a judgemental experience, where the inspectors deliver their verdict.

Oral feedback to the staff as a whole

In eight out of the 12 cases, the inspectors met with the whole staff to feed back their findings. Two of the four cases where a full staff debriefing did not occur were LEA review inspections whose procedures did not provide for such a meeting. The remaining two were both conducted in accordance with the Ofsted framework where, again, the procedures do not call for such a meeting. Nevertheless, two of the Ofsted-style inspections did include staff debriefing. In both cases, the lead inspector used his discretion to hold staff meetings. In one case, this was because the lead inspector felt that 'the staff as a whole should know the score', particularly as he appeared to have little faith in the headteacher to convey 'important messages about underachievement'. In the other, the lead inspector felt that 'the curriculum expertise lay with the staff' so he wanted them to hear the feedback directly. In all the other cases, the idea of holding a staff meeting appears to have been a given part of the procedure, perhaps emanating again from an intuitive commitment to a democratic principle.

The lead inspector's approach to these meetings appears often to have been similar to that adopted in the formal feedback to the head. The inspector outlined the findings of the inspection to a virtually silent gathering of the staff. However, it did not always go smoothly. This is how one inspector described what happened: 'I was apprehensive about how to make it worthwhile, somewhat intimidated. We had not prepared. The head did not provide a very good introduction. You could sense the atmosphere – it wasn't comfortable! We got some life into the meeting by teachers venting – not necessarily their own feelings, but for each other. Some staff were obviously not going to contribute anything – you could tell from their gestures and position that they were resentful – hostile even.'

This was one of two cases where the meeting became more than a simple presentation by the lead inspector to the staff. In this case, the lead inspector appeared to have been hoping for some kind of dialogue. However, when he invited the staff to comment, a discussion never developed. Teachers contributed separate comments in a highly charged emotional atmosphere. One of the teachers commented afterwards that people 'really wanted to talk and get things off their chest' but somehow they found it hard to break the ice.

In the second of these cases, the lead inspector's reading through of the inspection findings was interrupted by an outburst from a senior teacher who felt that she had been unjustly criticised. The lead inspector, who appears to have alienated herself from the staff at her previous meeting with them – when she had briefed them about the inspection – retorted: 'I'm sorry, but that's tough.' This response featured in everyone's memory of the inspection.

The particular teacher involved in this exchange was one of those whose work was least appreciated by the inspection team. In almost every case, the teachers with the weakest practice seem to have created a real difficulty for the inspection teams. In the full staff meeting, the difficulty of handling professional judgement in a human context has proved to be at its sharpest. These meetings have also revealed a more general intensity of emotion.

Reporting: negotiated reporting

In the period between the publication of the Audit Commission Report (1989) on quality assurance in local education authorities and the passing of the 1992 Education (Schools) Act, several LEAs looked for ways of developing the earlier work that had been done on school self-evaluation by evolving procedures for audited self-review as part of their overall monitoring arrangements. There was a strong emphasis on inspection 'with', as opposed to inspection 'of', presumably to sustain a developmental emphasis alongside the accountability of judgemental inspection asked for by the Audit Commission.

In two of the case studies which preceded the advent of the Ofsted framework, the idea of negotiation was put forward explicitly by the inspectors and in a third there was a strong suggestion of it. In one of these cases, the inspectors suggested that the report should be written jointly with the teachers. Their thinking appears to have been that the ultimate judgemental position was secure – the school was performing to at least a satisfactory level – and that to write the report with the staff would ensure their full ownership of the developmental issues. Unfortunately, key members of staff moved to other schools and the report was never actually written. The headteacher appears not to have been entirely happy with the arrangement anyway; he strongly criticised the way in which the inspectors switched so completely from a judgemental to a developmental agenda.

In another of these cases, the lead inspector was keen not only to offer a 'right of reply' but also to stimulate the teachers' response. The staff was offered the chance to write a response to the inspection reports, but they chose not to. One teacher said that she 'couldn't see what it would achieve'.

Although one of the inspectors in the third of these cases had undergone training in the use of the Ofsted framework, the lead inspector, who had not had such training, was prepared to discuss with the headteacher how the wording of the report would most support the meanings which the inspectors wished to put across. Here, there was little sense that the inspectors' findings would be changed, but negotiation was more openly allowed than in most other cases.

It could now be argued that these three instances have proved to be historical curiosities but I am not sure that this would be an appropriate conclusion. In one of the cases undertaken by HMI in accordance with the Ofsted framework, there was a clear sense that part of the purpose of the feedback to subject coordinators, prior to the completion of the inspection visit, was to check out whether the inspectors' view of the school 'would be acceptable' to the teachers. This could have meant that the inspectors wanted the teachers to agree with their findings, or it might have meant that they wanted to find out where their verdict would be most tested. It was probably a bit of both.

When, in this same case, the lead inspector told the headteacher that he could correct factual inaccuracies but could not argue with the judgements, there was little sense of negotiation. However, in subtle ways, negotiation had already taken place. There seems to have been a fine line between 'leakage' and negotiation.

Corrections were made to draft inspection reports. In two cases, wordings were renegotiated, in both cases in ways which softened the impact without changing the meaning. In one case, however, the headteacher missed an inaccuracy during his debriefing. By the time the inspectors met with the staff, the report was close to publication and could not be amended. The teachers were upset that, although they were told that they could tell the governors about the inaccuracy when the report was formally presented, a misrepresentation would be 'on the record'.

In all the cases, there seemed to be agreement that part of the rationale behind taking the headteacher through what the inspection report would contain was to ensure that there would be no factual inaccuracies. Did more fundamental alterations occur in the inspectors' judgements? A strong suggestion has emerged from the research interviews that the reports have been 'tailored' to match what the school 'is ready to hear'. This was not open negotiation, but a kind of shadow negotiation.

In one case, one inspector said that criticisms of the headteacher were 'withheld'. A colleague explained that the report was 'definitely tailored to the school's readiness'. This attitude recurred in another case where the lead inspector said that to criticise the head more strongly 'would have served no useful purpose'. This might suggest that the inspectors' developmental agenda can win out over a judgemental agenda. Alternatively it might suggest that human sympathy could temper hard-edged criticism.

There was a case where the inspectors were particularly unhappy about the performance of the teachers in one of the four year teams. They felt that it would have presented an unfair picture of the school if this poor practice were fully represented in the report. They chose only to allude to 'weaker practice' in the report but to tell the headteacher 'unofficially' that this is what they had chosen to do. This action probably stemmed from a human agenda – a desire to sustain the overall morale of the school – rather than from a developmental one. Nevertheless, they were making a judgement about how far they could report their negative judgements before their positive judgements would be undermined.

Although there were inspectors who were adamant that they would not 'withhold' things 'which need to be said in the interests of the children', there was a suggestion, even in the most judgemental form of inspection – an Ofsted inspection carried out by HMI – that the inspectors' real verdict on the school may not have been fully reported. In this case, the lead inspector broke with usual procedure and met with the staff so that he could tell them explicitly what would be implicit in the report. In one of the earlier case studies, which pre-dated the advent of the Ofsted framework, the inspectors wrote a report where they reported their positive comments explicitly but their negative comments almost entirely implicitly. At the end of the research period, despite the tightening of procedures in the Ofsted framework, the same reluctance to put negative findings into print seems to have persisted.

The care taken by the inspectors to *tell* the headteacher about poor practice of the teachers in a particular year group, rather than to report it in print, has been replicated elsewhere. Indeed, in almost every case, the lead inspector has left the headteacher in no doubt about which teachers in the school have the weakest practice. Most of the cases have had a 'worst' teacher, who has often proved to be a kind of scapegoat. What is significant here is that, procedurally, there has been an almost universal breaking of the principle that no teacher will be identified individually. The principle has been carried out to the letter, in that no individual teacher has been identified in print (though several have been identifiable to those who know the school), but not in spirit. This is important because it helps to explain the strong personal sense of accountability that teachers feel. In several cases, the inspectors felt strongly that a teacher 'needed to be taken on'. They have said so and other members of the staff, though not always the teacher directly involved, often seem to have been aware that they have done so.

Reporting: inspectors at work

Besides the explicit or implicit negotiation of its contents with the school, the report had to be put together by, or on behalf of, the inspection team. The central part of this process, the agreeing of the report's main findings and key recommendations, generally occurred when the team was still at the school. The actual writing of the report appears to have been left to one person, usually the lead inspector.

In the inspections carried out under HMI or Ofsted procedures, the report seems to have been collated from a collection of paragraphs written by all the inspectors in the team. The lead inspector has had the task of ensuring that the style of the report as a whole was consistent. Under HMI procedures, the reports were then checked by 'readers'. There was some mild resentment from HMI that their well-turned phrases were altered or edited out, particularly when they had taken care to write things in such a way that the school would understand.

In two of the LEA review inspections, the reports were also compiled from the contributions of the separate members of the team. In both of these cases there were problems because one of the team did not submit his sections on time. Indeed, in one of these cases, one of the team never wrote his contribution and the lead inspector had to do so on his behalf. In the other, there was tension because the team contained the senior inspector. The lead inspector appears to have felt insecure about this and suggested that the senior inspector had not gone out of his way to make the situation easier.

In the remaining cases, the report was written by one person on behalf of the whole team. There were several suggestions that what had resulted did not quite match the perceptions of the whole team. There was one particular case where two women members of the team felt that there were significant gender issues to report. The lead inspector chose not to report these. It was not clear whether this was because he had a particularly close professional relationship with the headteacher (he was the attached adviser to the school) or because he did not see the same significance in the issue. This instance, along with comments made in other cases, demonstrates another aspect of the key role played by the lead inspector. Equally, it demonstrates the extent to which the processes of inspection are dependent on judgement. The lead inspector has had to use his or her judgement to decide how the different perceptions of the team should be represented. The fact that none of the inspectors in the case studies had worked in the same team together before would have made this particularly difficult. Although one team related how they had 'spent hours' arguing about wordings, in general the time constraints of the inspection process meant that the final content and shape of the report were left to the judgement of one key person.

In this chapter and in the previous chapter, the emphasis has been on the technical performance and procedures of inspection. Whether inspection has been perceived as judgemental or developmental, the cases researched have followed similar patterns. Inspectors have formed judgements from evidence which has been collected from documentation, work-sampling, interviews and classroom observation and have reported back, orally and in writing. The methods the inspectors have used and the consistency with which they have used them appear to have affected the extent to which teachers and headteachers have accepted the inspectors' findings.

However, it has proved almost impossible to separate the technical aspects of inspection from the human. Repeatedly, in describing the way in which inspections have been carried out and in outlining the particular functions of the people involved, the presence of a range and depth of feelings has been obvious. The cases have been full of contrasting and conflicting perceptions and interpretations; inspectors and teachers have repeatedly alluded to their mutual relationships. These are now explored.

6 PATTERNS OF EMOTIONAL RESPONSE

This chapter explores the human aspects of inspection more specifically. I shall identify more patterns and contrasts; look for explanations for the strong feelings which have often been generated; and examine the ways in which people have consequently attempted to manage these feelings.

The emotional impact of inspection on teachers and headteachers

Just as there have been considerable similarities in the procedures followed in each of the inspections, so too have patterns emerged in the emotional responses of headteachers, teachers and inspectors.

When schools first heard about the inspections, there was a strong sense of 'bad news'. One teacher described how her headteacher 'came in looking ashen, asking what is the worst thing that can happen' and a headteacher described how the teachers' 'hearts sank to the bottom of their boots'. This initial reaction, which was reported by teachers in almost every case, seems to have been related to the mythology of inspection and to the idea of teachers being 'victims' of the process. Teachers have repeatedly referred to other schools or colleagues who had had bad experiences of inspection and, in just two cases, mentioned their own previous negative experiences.

The immediate emotional reaction to the notification of inspection seems to have given way to a widespread sense of apprehension. Words such as 'tension', 'fear', 'anxiety', 'nervousness', 'up-tight', 'wound up', 'petrified', and 'suspense' have abounded. Rarely has anyone within the school described the period of preparation between the first notification of the inspection and the actual arrival of the inspectors in positive terms. There was just one teacher who felt a 'buzz' as the staff prepared for the inspection and there have been references in several case studies to joking and humour amongst the staff, particularly immediately before the start of the inspection visit, but these references have had a stronger sense of gallows humour than of eager anticipation of what was to come.

The picture that has been presented across the 12 case studies has suggested the run-up to the first night of an important theatrical performance. Some actors have experienced major pre-performance nervousness, bordering on real stage fright, whilst others have managed to be more relaxed. People have adopted their own little rituals to help them to feel more in control, such as meticulous lesson preparation or new wall displays. Just as the director of a play might circulate among the cast before the performance trying to calm the actors' worst fears, so too has the headteacher worked hard to 'manage morale' and 'relieve tension'.

Each individual teacher has felt exposed to the impending scrutiny of the inspectors, just as, presumably, even the bit-part player on stage might dread being panned by a major critic. One teacher described himself as speculating, 'would a bad day affect your career?' At the same time, teachers have been very supportive of one another as they have recognised that it is the collective performance which will be judged and reported. This has brought out a solid arity with one another and often substantial loyalty towards the headteacher – the show's director.

The power of the major theatre critics is legendary. One facet of this is the sense that the actor is at the mercy of the critic, who can make or break a reputation. This power relationship has been a significant feature of inspection. From the outset of the inspection – 'it was time our number came up'; 'we were the ones picked out of the hat' – through to the report at the end – 'we'd hoped that they'd temper it with mercy' – there has repeatedly been the suggestion of the teachers as victims.

As the teachers have prepared to perform at their best for the inspector, there has been a lot of pride at stake. Teachers have wanted to be seen to be doing a 'professional job'. They have been anxious that things might go wrong, and apprehensive about what the inspectors might say, particularly since the teachers have sometimes not known exactly what the inspectors would be looking for.

One particular fear which has surfaced in several cases has been that the teacher would lose control in the classroom. As we saw earlier, there was some evidence that teachers arranged an artificially 'safe' provision in the classroom. In two cases in particular, 'there were anxieties about how the children might respond', and in another, there were several references to organisational arrangements, such as tuning the orchestra, which might 'go wrong'.

One headteacher expressed some surprise at the apprehension his staff had felt. In trying to explain it, he suggested three points: 'the discomfort of somebody watching your lessons'; 'a basic insecurity – there have been too many negative messages [in the media]'; and 'the stereotype HMI brings out the worst – he wills the school to do something wrong'. This latter point, with its reference to the mythological stereotype of the inspector, matches the idea of the legendary theatre critic. All three points relate to the teachers' confidence. Confidence appears to have been a key factor in the variety of teachers' feelings immediately prior to and during the inspection visit. Confidence has not necessarily been related to competence. As was hinted by more than one headteacher, 'those who worried most were those who didn't need to'. This may have been because the more reflective teachers had a greater awareness of all that the inspectors might look for or find. It was one such teacher who summed up the sense of waiting to go on stage: 'It got to the point where we just wanted it over.'

Once the inspection visits were under way, the emotional response of different teachers, even in the same school, has varied significantly. Again, confidence appears to have been the key. 'One person's perception of a grilling is another's perception of a stimulating dialogue.' This experience of interviews was replicated in the classroom: 'The staff did warm to some more than others – I think this made a difference to their confidence.' In the interests of professionalism, some teachers seem to have been prepared to put up with a lot: 'It's good to be put under pressure.'

A consequence of low confidence has been a tendency to be defensive. In one particular case, teachers seemed to be attempting to avoid the inspectors: 'a teacher suddenly timetabled a student to teach when we [the inspectors] were on our way. Another didn't bring planning documents on purpose.' This happened in other cases; in one 'the school was successful at holding us at a distance'; and in another the headteacher's blocking behaviour raised questions of 'who was managing whom' in the inspection. This defensiveness intensified when teachers began to deal with negative criticism.

Teachers' familiarity with being watched seems to have affected their confidence. Several younger teachers have mentioned that they were used to being watched and so the inspection was not as daunting as it might otherwise have been. One more experienced teacher pointed out that she enjoyed performing to an audience and actually 'looked forward' to the inspectors' visits – 'I enjoy being watched – I'm confident in the children's ability and mine.' One inspector has suggested that inspection constitutes an invasion of teachers' territory: 'The classroom is their domain, they feel very vulnerable.' Whilst a teacher in this same case agreed that 'people don't like having people in their classrooms', this notion of invasion has not surfaced explicitly in any of the other cases. It is possible that this inspector's perception related as much to his insecurity as a visitor as it did to the teacher's perception of his arrival. Nevertheless, this notion is close to the suggestion of several inspectors that the teachers are vulnerable to 'attack'. It also fits with the way that teachers' defensiveness seems to have intensified as they have been confronted by views of their school and their practice which do not match those they previously held.

An emotional side-effect of the anxiety of 'being watched' has been the disappointment felt by some teachers when the inspectors have failed to appear

– 'Nobody came in! It felt a bit of a let-down.' However, this feeling has not been widely expressed and has as often been matched by a sense of being overvisited: 'They were in and out all the time. I certainly felt as if my practice had been well and truly looked at.'

The intensity of the inspection period has been a consistent feature of every case. In one case, the lead inspector commented that 'the staff were utterly drained – they were having to keep up an act'; in another, a teacher said that 'I'd had enough by the third day – the constant looking out [for the inspectors] was a mental pressure.' In several cases, it was suggested that the children as well as the teachers were getting tired as the week went on, particularly on the third and fourth days: 'By Wednesday we were tired out and weren't able to shrug things off. Everyone was going over the top.'

The headteacher's behaviour during the inspection was directly related to the emotional climate. There have been frequent references to the head's attempts to manage morale – 'the head was being very jolly'. Headteachers often betrayed the tension they felt – 'he was pacing up and down'– or were seen as trying to hide it – 'he was stalwartly calm'. In two cases, the headteacher had wanted to impress on the inspectors how 'difficult' the school's catchment was to pre-empt criticism and protect the school.

This sense of wanting to put one's excuses before the inspectors pronounced their findings suggested a certain pessimism about what the inspectors themselves would think. This pervasive fear of disaster has surfaced in almost every case. There were casualties after the inspections, but during the inspections themselves, people's worst nightmares were rarely realised. We have heard of interviews which felt like interrogations, and of discomfort caused by the insensitivity of inspectors in classrooms, but comments such as: 'we tried to make the odd joke with the children but it fell flat and we felt silly – it was absolutely awful' have been rare.

Perhaps because teachers and headteachers have been left bruised and scarred by inspections, and, as one headteacher put it, 'I've heard of headteachers being eased out', the negative associations of inspection are understandable. Certainly the sense that 'we were being done' surfaced again and again: 'I expected them to look for faults – it's easier to criticise than to praise'; 'we've been "subjected" – yes that's a good word for it'; 'there's an expectation of it being painful'; 'everyone assumes the negative'. During the inspection, this feeling was compounded by a general lack of feedback, particularly to those whose practice the inspectors felt less happy about. This left teachers with a sense that something was wrong, sometimes even when nothing was: 'The hardest part was trying to work out what they were thinking – they didn't say much.' The fact that teachers often felt that the inspectors were controlling the agenda added to the negativity: 'We had no shared view of what the expectations of the review team would be.'

The inspectors themselves repeatedly used language which showed how aware they were of the situation: 'I didn't want the staff to feel they were being victimised'; 'there's a feeling of threat, like we're going to jump on them with claws and fangs!'; 'we're not trying to catch people out'; 'the staff felt more battered than I expected them to be – they felt they'd been hung out to dry'; 'we weren't going to hang anyone'; 'it's almost as if someone had asked them to create a beefsteak and had marked it as a cheese soufflé'. It is reasonable to suggest that if this is the imagery that inspectors use when discussing their work, it is hardly surprising that inspection carries negative connotations. It is possible also that it is in inspectors' interests to generate some sense of fear – to protect their own vulnerabilities.

As the inspection visits moved towards their completion, the teachers' worst fears were sometimes realised. Rather more often, their fears were allayed. The emotional impact at the end of the inspections has taken two forms: a massive sense of relief that the special performance had finished, and reaction to the inspectors' findings. The extent of the release of emotion at the end of the inspections demonstrates the intensity of the experience as a whole. One teacher talked of 'catharsis' and several described celebrations, often accompanied by champagne, at the end of the inspection week. This release was accompanied for many by tiredness and exhaustion: 'we were drained out at the end – like a tap left running'.

The emotional impact of inspections seems to have lingered for some in the form of what one headteacher called 'post-inspection syndrome'. This head said, 'I knew it was going to knock my self-esteem. Afterwards, I felt that I couldn't do anything for a week, and then I felt very deskilled – now I'm back to equilibrium.' One of her staff, speaking some weeks after the inspection, felt that 'it threw her [the head] more than we thought it would. She has not bounced back as quickly as I'd have expected.' This situation was repeated in another case: 'At the time it flattened the staff – a deadening hand, like a big smack. It took about six weeks to get out of it. That was in a school where things were OK – what if there had been criticisms?' In a further case, the effect was related to staff morale: 'It was extremely destructive of staff morale – it engendered mistrust, backbiting, blaming.' There were also teachers who experienced significant breakdowns in their health.

A more sustained emotional impact did not occur in every case or for every teacher. Some saw the inspection as something which 'came and went', and asked 'what were we so bothered about?' What allows one teacher to say that 'it blew over very quickly. I'd forgotten it shortly afterwards' whilst the same school's head talked of a six-week recovery period?

The answer to this question seems to lie in the different perceptions of the significance of the inspection and its findings. This teacher who felt little lasting impact had felt confident going into the inspection and had not felt personally implicated in any of its findings. Her comments suggested that the inspection had not prompted much personal reflection. Ironically, this was the very teacher about whose practice the inspectors had felt most negative. Another teacher in the same inspection had expected more from it: 'I was rather hurt not to be mentioned in the report. It has altered me – I have reduced my commitment – some level of demotivation – but I wouldn't want that to cloud what was a good review of the school.' She agreed with the headteacher that 'immediately post-review we experienced a disorientation'.

This variety of response at the end of inspections emphasises the extent to which the whole process has been subject to the individual perceptions of the participants. The extent of the exhaustion and the length of the recovery period suggest that for different people the stakes were higher. They invested more in their 'performance', either because they had higher professional expectations or because they lacked confidence. But there was also a variety of emotions which related to what was said by the inspectors and, despite the apparent disintegration in the staff referred to above, there was more generally a strengthening of staff solidarity.

Not surprisingly, teachers and headteachers who felt that they had received good notices from the inspectors experienced raised morale, whilst those who had been criticised were hurt and defensive and looked for ways to displace what had been said. As one headteacher put it: 'Bits lifted the teachers and others pushed them down – there was negative reinforcement of negative practice.'

In the research interviews as a whole, the balance of comment about reactions to the inspectors' findings has been strongly weighted towards the negative. There were just three references in this context to improved confidence and morale. The negative weighting may reflect teachers' more negative expectations of the whole inspection process. If teachers perceived themselves as having escaped the criticism they feared, then perhaps there will have been less to make comment about. Alternatively, it is likely that teachers found it more difficult to talk about success – a positive self-image is not a general feature of the teaching profession.

Whilst several teachers have attempted to displace the validity of the inspectors' findings by criticising their procedures, their more direct references to the inspectors' findings have often been characterised by tension, loss of confidence and a lowering of morale, and occasionally by anger. Two headteachers in particular were unable to describe their reactions to the inspectors' findings without considerable feeling. One had been irritated by the inspectors' idiosyncratic use of language; their unwillingness to substantiate their judgements with evidence; and by an unexplained change of emphasis in the inspection itself. In the other case, the head's anger seemed to stem from several sources: a disappointment that the inspectors had not been more complimentary; a sense that the timing of the inspection and the issues raised were inconvenient; and, perhaps, a difficulty in adjusting to a more judgemental emphasis in inspection and advisory practice.

As far as teachers have been concerned, how might we expect anyone to react when their professional practice has been criticised? If the person concerned has sufficient confidence to be able to accept criticism as constructive to future improvement, then perhaps no offence need be taken: 'It has given me a personal shot in the arm to take the next step – after the exhaustion and feeling that I don't know if I can do this.' But if the person hopes for validation, perhaps against his or her own better judgement, then the potential for hurt pride and lost confidence is substantial. One teacher echoed the irritation of the headteacher who may have been having difficulty adjusting to the new climate of accountability: 'I became quite angry, defensive. How can anyone come in here and criticise?'

The comments made in research interviews have suggested that a sense of 'fairness' has played a significant part: 'people were very up-tight about criti-cisms if they felt they were unjustified'; 'when I read the report, it was spot on – completely fair, but it was the last straw for C—.' This comment, while emphasising fairness, points up a persistent feature of teachers' approach to the inspection report: they seem to have gone through the inspectors' com-ments with a fine tooth comb looking for themselves: 'It was the identifiable personal comments which aroused deep feelings.' There are three ironies here. One is that the inspectors seem to have gone to great lengths to emphasise that it has been the school, not the individual teachers, that has been under scrutiny. The convention of not identifying teachers in reports has not ex-plicitly been broken in any of the cases researched. The second is that teachers have sometimes identified themselves with comments which did not apply to them. The third is that there have been cases where the teachers at whom the strongest criticisms were implicitly aimed have not identified themselves with these criticisms. At the same time, the prevalence of unofficial feedback and 'scapegoats' in the case studies suggests that teachers were entirely jus-tified in personalising their scrutiny of the inspection reports.

The responses of individuals to the inspectors' findings, particularly those perceived as critical, have sometimes been swallowed up in the way that staffs as a whole have reacted. In one case, two of the inspection team fed back to a staff meeting. Apparently, 'the staff had a strong desire to get their feelings off their chest', but, despite the attempts by the lead inspector to encourage the teachers to 'vent' their feelings, the release of emotion never took place. Instead, there was a series of queries about points in the report, implicitly challenging the inspectors' findings. A teacher admitted that in one of these exchanges 'the staff supported a teacher who was criticised, even though they agreed with the criticism'. This presents a picture of the teachers joining forces against external attack, with an emotional response sufficiently strong to undercut a rational position.

This has proved to be an extreme example of a general feature of inspec-tions: an increase in staff solidarity. Apart from the one case already referred to, several teachers and headteachers have mentioned how the inspection has brought staff together. One headteacher also felt that 'The relationship between staff and governors became much closer.' This seems to reflect the notion of invasion suggested earlier; the school has united against a perceived threat. It seems also sometimes to have been related to a loyalty to the head-teacher. There were two cases where teachers explicitly claimed that they 'did not want to let the head down'.

In one school, the staff met together at the end of each day during the inspection: 'People shared worries and the positive side. The meetings were very valuable. In the run-up we'd hardly talked to each other.' This reveals a third possible explanation for an increase in staff solidarity: the carrying out of a project together, particularly when everyone has been subject to the same imperative, is likely to have had a strong team-building effect. However, people have been left isolated from the staff team; there have been casualties in the process.

A particular form of isolation emerged in one case. A teacher was seen by his colleagues as having laid on a special performance for the inspectors which was inconsistent with his usual practice. The fact that his practice was identifiably praised by the inspectors caused considerable resentment. His colleagues understandably felt that this was unfair. At the same time, this instance suggested that there was an edge of competitiveness in the way that the teachers were looking for validation from the inspectors. Interestingly, competition has not surfaced as a general issue for teachers, although there have been hints of it in inspection teams.

If teachers have felt personally judged in inspections, it would be reasonable to expect that they might compare their performances. In the research interviews, teachers have often alluded to colleagues they know to have been criticised. Apart from the one instance mentioned, there has been no trace of resentment towards colleagues who might have been seen as more successful. This may be because their preoccupation has been with 'passing' rather than being put into any kind of rank order, or it may be because the teachers interviewed would not have considered it seemly to reveal any resentment which was driven essentially by jealousy. The process of unofficial feedback by which problematic teaching was brought to the attention of the headteacher did also identify particularly strong performers. Very little seems to have been made of this information. Likewise, if teachers did have the information to identify either themselves or others as stronger performers, they did not generally allude to it. In one case, a teacher was encouraged to put herself forward for promotion, but this was the only other occasion where any teacher was clearly credited with positive practice. Teachers could be identified with the subjects they were responsible for coordinating. There were instances where they admitted disappointment when a subject was 'only' described as satisfactory, as opposed to good.

It has been clear that the inspections have generated a strong emotional response. The compressed and time-constrained nature of the inspection process has served only to intensify this response. There has been little relief: teachers have commented on the stress of being interviewed in their breaks and, in a few cases, of having to 'entertain' their inspector-visitors in the staffroom. As one teacher put it, 'it is like an exam'. Although there have been as many different responses as there have been individuals involved, and although there have been fluctuations in the emotional temperature, there does seem to have been an overall pattern. The pre-inspection period has been characterised more by anxiety and uncertainty than by excitement and anticipation as the school has prepared to perform as well as it knows how. The inspection period has been characterised by the sustained tension, fed by adrenaline, of being 'on stage', with the gathering exhaustion of a marathon. Unlike a stage performance, the actors have had the additional complication and intensity of having to interact with their critics. This has sometimes reassured and sometimes undermined confidence. Inevitably, the completion of the inspection has been accompanied by some kind of an emotional release. There has been a strong sense of exhaustion. For example, one teacher described the feedback meeting between staff and inspector as 'flat and an anticlimax – an emotional disappointment'. This emotional disappointment has been compounded for some by the perceived negativity of the inspectors' findings whilst for a few there has been a 'boost to their self-esteem' and morale.

The emotional impact on inspectors

Whilst the teachers have been on their emotional roller-coaster, the inspectors have had feelings of their own. My attempts to make sense of these feelings has been complicated by the interrelationship between emotions and perceptions. Different teachers have reacted differently to the same event, comment or person because they have interpreted it differently. They appear to have interpreted it according to their sense of self-confidence and self-esteem, particularly as professionals – a point to which I shall return. In general, inspectors have been less forthcoming about their own emotional response than they have been about their perceptions of the school. They have articulated rather more about the feelings they have seen in others than those they have felt in themselves.

Inspectors also have levels of self-confidence and self-esteem. However, there has been a subtle difference in their responses which may have been related to the different role they have played in the inspection process. Inspectors and teachers are all people; people all have emotions and perceptions. But in the context of an inspection, the inspector is, in a grammatical sense, the subject and the teacher the object: the inspector inspects – judges – the teacher. Whatever the rhetoric of the inspector who looks to inspect 'with' the school, the harsh reality has been that, even when the inspection has been invited by the school, the process has placed the school 'in the dock' with the inspector 'on the bench'.

So the patterns of feeling which have been articulated by the inspectors in my research have been akin to the ebb and flow of a courtroom where feelings relate to the changes in perception of what the ultimate verdict might be as new evidence is brought to light. Other situations in which a measured judgement is called for come to mind: it has been suggested that interviewers make up their mind about a candidate for a job within the first two minutes of the interview and then only see (perceive) evidence during the remainder of the interview which confirms that initial judgement (Roberts 1985). As with an interview panel, the ultimate decisions of an inspection team have been complicated by the conflicting opinions (judgements) of the different team members.

The inspectors' descriptions of this ebb and flow have revealed two particular issues: a struggle for balance, and a consensus about individual teachers' competence.

As the inspectors have worked towards an overall summative judgement about the school, they have often described how their perceptions of what they have been seeing have been caught in a negative trap:

'At the end of day one we were struggling to find nice things to say about the school – this is normal, but there are usually some glimmers too.'

'When we met as a team we went down – got channelled into negatives – we had to snap out of that.'

'By the second day, the team was gung ho and ready to hang them up by their thumbs.'

'At one stage I was being sucked into the negative – the negative was not reversed – there was a negative hole on the Wednesday afternoon – we'd only gone in one direction.'

There seems to have been a strong awareness that the team must balance this out by the end of the inspection: 'On day two you usually get pretty low – picky and negative. By day four you begin to get a more balanced view. At the end of day one when we were at [another inspection] she [lead inspector] said "come on, let's not be negative".' At the same time, there has been a tension about which perception is the correct one: 'The team is often at its lowest point at the end of the first day. It could be that the first impression is the most realistic . . . I've also been on reviews where I've almost been frightened to be positive.'

These comments were meant to relate to judgements which were based on evidence. Yet we can detect the qualitative nature of what had to take place. The inspectors have described their progress towards judgement in emotional terms – 'lowest point', 'frightened', 'gung ho'. There has been an underlying commitment to 'balance' which is presumably about weighing evidence but which seems also to carry overtones of wanting to present positive findings which are at least equivalent to the negative.

The formulation of the 'corporate view' of the school can be seen to be a lot more than the mere calibrated measurement of quantities. There seems to have been a human desire to 'say nice things about the school' and there has been a potent interaction between members of the team: 'I felt that the group was consenting to a stereotype for each teacher.' However, this was not always the case: 'J— was forming his view more slowly; when he did speak he revealed the ways in which he was testing what had been said against criteria.' This idea of testing a perception did recur: 'We certainly saw some poor practice. For a couple of teachers, that perception did not change. For a couple of others, it improved steadily during the inspection.'

It would appear that the struggle for balance has been more carefully sustained in respect of the findings which relate to the school as a whole. The balance of judgement has not seemed as secure when inspectors have been considering individual teachers. A comment such as 'that was the worst lesson I've ever seen' can result in a teacher becoming a casualty of the process, even though there would be no specific mention of this teacher in the inspection report.

As well as sometimes appearing to be emotional in the process of reaching judgements, inspectors have also found themselves emotionally affected by what they have seen: 'then I moved on to the next class – I was devastated'; 'I was angry that the children were getting such a bum deal'.

Despite my having drawn attention to the stronger externalisation of feeling on the part of the inspectors, they have made some comments about their own emotional reactions. These have tended to relate to the inspectors' personal self-confidence. In a few cases, inspectors have talked of their anxiety about inspecting subjects other than their own specialism; some inspectors have been open about the difficulty of arriving at secure judgements based on a rather narrow evidence base; and one inspector in particular admitted to several teachers that, because of a certain 'shyness', he had great difficulty in establishing the kind of relationship he felt was needed.

There have also been several instances where inspectors have felt particularly insecure in relation to their colleagues. One inspector felt that he was an outsider in a team which otherwise knew each other well; he did not feel that his contributions were welcome. This sense of animosity also appeared in another case where an inspector cast considerable doubt on the reliability of one of his colleague's judgements and where the conduct of the lead inspector in leading team meetings was quite heavily criticised. It is not surprising that there was some friction in inspection teams given that the people concerned were often coming together for the first time. In contrast to air crews, who are repeatedly scheduled to work with different people, consistent procedures are not as clearly established; roles are not as well defined; and there is substantial scope for competing interpretations of evidence.

The tension and its consequent insecurity for inspectors within a team seems sometimes to have been exacerbated by gender, status and previous association with the school. In one case, the lead inspector was a woman in a team which was otherwise male. Several teachers in this case suggested that this might have contributed to her apparent nervousness which, they felt, had caused her to be 'sharp' and 'rude'. Given that there have been several other references by teachers to their preferences for being inspected by, sometimes, men or, at other times, women, this might as easily have been an issue external to the team as internal to it. However, the lead inspector herself referred several times to the difficulty of working with her senior inspector as part of the team. It seems more likely that her apparent irritability stemmed from the frustration of her not feeling able to manage the performance of this senior colleague as she might have wished. The fact that she had had previous contact with the school seems also to have unsettled her.

The gender issue did surface in relation to the dynamics of the inspection team in two other cases. In both, the lead inspector was a woman and there was the suggestion that she had felt it necessary to adopt a particularly assertive persona which appears to have 'grated' on some members of the team.

The status of the lead inspector has also been raised as an issue in several other cases. Two strands have emerged: leading a team which contains a senior colleague; and perceptions of the credibility of the lead inspector's leadership. It would appear that leading a team containing a senior colleague has put the lead inspector on his or her mettle, increasing the stress of the experience. Although one inspector mentioned that her senior colleague was 'always very supportive', she nevertheless had particularly wanted to 'get it right'.

In those cases where the usual hierarchy of inspectors had been reversed, the source of the lead inspector's insecurity was fairly obvious. The situation seems to have been more subtle where teachers and members of inspection teams have recognised leadership in someone other than the lead inspector or, in one case, where one member of the inspection team was seen by others as attempting to overrule the lead inspector – 'he had competing ways of doing things'. In this case, the lead inspector hinted that he was more irritated than undermined by this. In general however, whilst team inspectors have sometimes questioned or criticised the authority of the lead inspector, there has been little to suggest that the process has suffered significantly. Lead inspectors have frequently admitted insecurity but it has not been because they felt that their leadership was challenged. It has usually been because they wanted to 'do the job well'.

A certain seriousness and intensity has pervaded the inspectors' comments. At the same time, the research interviews did not explicitly ask inspectors, or indeed teachers, to say whether they enjoyed inspections. There was a strong dynamic in their responses towards the satisfaction of having done a 'proper job'. Nevertheless, there have been glimmers of lightness and humour. One inspector suggested that a factor in the success of an inspection was 'the team effort – working together as a team – laughing together as well as making corporate judgements'. Teachers have occasionally commented that the inspectors appeared to be enjoying themselves, particularly during the later stages of the inspection. One teacher commented that the inspectors were 'three happy people – they enjoyed their visit'.

7   RELATIONSHIPS

AND RITUALS

This chapter examines the relationships between teachers and inspectors. The particular factors of connection and gender are considered. The discussion moves on to look more closely at the part that ritual plays in inspection and how it affects the behaviour of the participants. The last part of the chapter considers a particularly significant outcome of the relationships and rituals of inspection: the scapegoats.

Relationships

Whilst a few teachers seem to have noticed the internal dynamics of the inspection teams, there has been no evidence that they attempted to exploit any of these tensions or divisions in order to displace the validity of the inspectors' findings. This contrasts with the way that they looked for mistakes in procedure. Indeed, when it has come to the human agenda, there has been a consistent one-sidedness about who might manage it. Teachers have commented at length on their opinions of how the inspectors have behaved and they have been aware of inspectors' feelings; but, when they have discussed their own feelings, they have talked of how they have reacted, suggesting that the inspectors were responsible for generating them. This reflects the pattern of inspectors being more forthcoming about the teachers' feelings than about their own and probably carries the same explanation – that the inspectors were the subject of the verb 'to inspect' and the teachers were the object. Put another way, the inspectors have had the power, the teachers have not. A general consequence of this has been that most in-spectors have chosen to invest considerable energy in establishing good relationships with the headteachers and teachers and to manage the emo-tional agendas.

The schools have also invested in their relationship with the inspectors. We saw earlier how they prepared carefully for their visitors. One inspector felt that 'the warmth of the welcome' from the school had been one of the main reasons why that inspection had gone so well. But, perhaps in keeping with house guests, the teachers have not been able to do a great deal to manage the inspectors once they have arrived. Three headteachers identified themselves as having tried to do so but they all acknowledged that they had not succeeded, although the inspectors in one of these cases felt that the headteacher had succeeded. One headteacher, who made no claim to have tried to manage the inspection, did prompt one of the inspectors to comment that 'It raised questions about who was managing whom.' He was sufficiently cavalier in failing to follow his side of the LEA's procedures that he succeeded in undermining the effectiveness of the inspectors. However, this rather negative example serves to prove the point: there has been an expectation that the inspectors will manage the inspection and the school has only really been able to stop that by subversion.

This point was underscored by teachers' comments in two other cases. One of them, when asked about a 'bad inspection' commented that it would be one where there was 'animosity from the staff and non-cooperation from the children'. It was interesting that this teacher chose to respond to this ques-tion from the inspectors' side of the story ('animosity from the staff') as well as her own ('non-cooperation from the children'). This situation was repeated when a teacher was asked about what makes a 'successful inspection'. Again, she suggested that it was 'when the teachers have not put the inspectors against the wall'.

We saw glimpses of this power of teachers to subvert inspections when a teacher left her planning at home and another (metaphorically) hid behind her student. So it could be argued that the teachers did manage their relation-ships with the inspectors by choosing to conform. However, this seems to confirm the essential passivity of the teachers in the face of the inspectors.

The idea of subversion was also used by an inspector, who suggested that she always wanted to 'subvert the aims of inspection to make it a positive experience' for the teachers. She went on to say that inspection was 'all about personal relationships'. In what way might she have seen inspection as being in opposition to personal relationships? To answer this, perhaps we need to return to what people have seen as the purposes for inspection. An HMI placed a powerful emphasis on cultivating relationships: 'I try to put myself in their place. I phone the head to soften the blow and introduce myself as a person. I try to put across the developmental outcome. I explain that I understand their fears – try to make them appreciate that colleagues will try to be unobtrusive. Terrified teachers find it difficult to relate. I'm looking for rapport. Teachers give far more – honesty about their work and their ques-tioning. They'll try to cover up if we are seen as a critical face.'

When pressed further on why he took such trouble to develop relationships, particularly when he had talked of colleagues who were often intentionally more formal in their dealings with teachers, he seemed uncertain. He concluded: 'Even if the relationship makes no difference, I'd still prefer to engage in a human process.' Whilst he was clearly entitled to his preference, it was perhaps unfair to question his intuitive emphasis on relationships. Surely the relationship does make a difference?

This inspector revealed that he wanted a 'developmental outcome'. He saw development as well as judgement in inspection. But even in the context of a judgemental inspection he gave good reason to manage positive relationships: teachers might have tried to cover up if they had been frightened. Since the gathering of evidence is fundamental to inspection, any withholding of evidence would have distorted his findings. Another inspector made the same point: 'You can disarm teachers by using their first names. I don't want to frighten people or keep them at a distance – getting them to engage with me is a way of getting the best information.'

So from a judgemental viewpoint, the quality of relationships makes a difference to the comprehensiveness and balance of the evidence available. This would perhaps be why there have been several references to 'trust', 'reassurance', 'making people feel relaxed', 'being natural' and to the general importance of 'relationships'. Eraut (1978) also emphasises the importance of trust in his research into educational evaluation. We have heard how teachers have felt constrained in their classrooms with the more 'starchy' inspectors, which may have undermined the acceptability of the inspectors' subsequent findings.

If inspection is seen from a developmental viewpoint, the significance of relationships takes on another dimension. When inspectors have talked about development, they have also been looking for teachers to accept and take ownership of the inspection findings. This was one of their concerns about feedback. They have also talked of 'leakage' and, in particular, of needing to match what they reported to 'what the school was ready to hear'. When relationships have not been quite right, then the communication of findings has been in jeopardy. A teacher referred to the failure of the lead inspector to secure acceptance of the inspection findings in the follow-up staff meeting: 'When I read the report, I thought it was spot on. But if you haven't got the right manner to get it across, you've lost everything. She [the lead inspector] was rude and never smiled.'

This problem can extend to the acceptability of the written report itself. One teacher commented that 'the report wasn't wrong, the emphasis was'. He commented later that 'it was brutal but fair'. But he was clearly asserting that this brutality had made it difficult, if not impossible, for some of his colleagues to accept the findings.

The more that inspection is viewed formatively, the more the idea of learning comes into play. The place of reflection in the inspection process will be considered in more detail later, but it would appear that there were teachers who found that they could put themselves alongside the inspectors and engage in professional discussion. One teacher commented how she had come 'to understand how A— [an inspector] sees things and I learned a lot from him'; and an inspector touched a similar point when she claimed, 'I give advice as well – I've got to be human about this. If it's a conversation, then advice is an inevitable part of it.'

Unfortunately, some teachers experienced a conversation as an interrogation. It does not seem to be sufficient to say that relationships have been important or significant in inspections. We need to be clear as to what kind of relationship has been involved. In the earlier stages of the research, there seemed to be significance in whether or not inspectors and teachers felt that they were 'on the same side'. In one case there was a distinct 'them and us' situation which developed during the inspection in opposite directions: some felt that the teachers and inspectors grew further apart, and some that the 'gap' was closed. In two other cases one headteacher saw the inspectors as 'colleagues', and the other asserted that 'we're all on the same side'. In both of these cases, the teachers did not have quite the same fellow feeling. Although references to this idea have persisted – 'I saw one inspector as a foe, but two were supportive and I was able to discuss things with them' – the belief that there might be a correlation between the 'success' of an inspection and the closure of any 'gap' seems out of place.

I contend that there is a subject–object relationship which is intrinsic to inspection. However, this relationship can take several forms. Drawing on the constructs of transactional analysis (Harris 1973), we can identify differences between relationships which are 'level' and relationships which are 'vertical'. Transactional analysis suggests that many transactions resemble the relationship between a parent and a child: the blaming or accusative 'parent' elicits either an adaptive or a rebellious (defensive) response from the 'child'. Likewise, the nurturing parent 'rescues' the defenceless child:

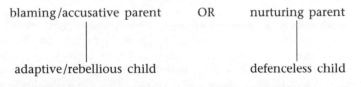

These are power relationships and can be seen to be hierarchical or 'vertical'. When transferred to grown-ups, the transactions may look like this:

In the context of inspection, the teacher may see the inspector as the judgemental 'persecutor' and may respond as a victim. This resonates in the feelings of the teacher who felt 'like a child who is asked but cannot answer' and of the headteacher who was angry with herself for sounding 'just like a guilty child who hasn't done her homework'.

Transactional analysts argue that the only kind of learning which can easily occur in this vertical relationship is conditioning. This would elicit the kind of 'strategic compliance' that Professor Alexander found in his research (1991) into the work of advisers in Leeds. For learning to occur, the learner needs to be active in processing information and experience – evidence. This requires a 'level' transaction between 'adults':

adult ————————————————————— adult

Such a transaction requires a certain equality between the two people involved. If the inspector has the given status of his or her role, which carries positional power and may also carry the authority of expertise (Handy 1976), then the self-confidence required by the teacher to reach a position alongside (level with) the inspector is substantial. Conversely, if inspectors attempt to divest themselves of their power and status, they may have to do so demonstratively if they are to convince less confident teachers that they are approachable and accessible – only human.

The nature of the relationships in the cases studied has more frequently fitted the parent–child 'vertical' than the adult–adult 'level' transaction. Either way, the notion of closing a gap seems inappropriate: the inspector cannot take the place of the teacher, nor can the inspector-as-teacher take the place of the teacher-as-learner.

We have seen numerous examples of the persecutor–victim relationship. Whenever teachers have felt defensive they may have been responding from a position of low self-esteem. And wherever inspectors have been 'sharp' or 'rude' there has been the suggestion that the inspector has adopted a position where the object of his or her criticism has appeared as less than 'OK' (or conversely, that the inspectors' own self-esteem was low).

The idea of the inspector as 'nurturer' has also recurred in people's comments, most frequently in the context of 'reassurance'. It has also surfaced in the protectiveness which inspectors seem often to have felt towards the school and which headteachers have often felt towards the teachers. The fine line between inspectors successfully matching their feedback to the school's readiness and withholding more negative criticism, for fear of offence, has sometimes been crossed. As one inspector asked: 'How do you deal with a minority of teachers who make a school vulnerable without destroying the confidence of all the teachers there?'

In this particular case, although the lead inspector identified the quality of teaching as probably the most important issue for the school, the message had been left so understated in the reporting that it had not got through. There have been other examples where this tailoring has led to unpalatable messages being withheld in reports.

This suggestion of protectiveness also appeared as an explanation for not giving teachers oral feedback – the teachers might have been upset by it. A further example of this occurred when an inspector found herself having to cope with practice that had discomfited her. She chose to ask 'gentle questions . . . I made no comment about the quality, that would have been too destructive.'

However, it would be a mistake to take the persecutor–victim or nurturer–victim scenario too far. Inspectors have often been faced with difficult situations. They have confronted practice which they have felt was unacceptable and have had to decide very quickly what to do about it. The process of inspection may involve gathering evidence, forming a judgement and feeding it back, but consistently there seems to have been something which has mediated the messages which the evidence would, in a purely functional way, have generated. There has been a pervasive consciousness amongst both inspectors and teachers of the consequences of their interactions. In one case all of the inspectors made some reference to the fact that they felt that their disappointment at what they were finding must have 'communicated itself to the staff' in some way, 'adding to the reaction and anxiety'. In another case a teacher commented that inspectors conveyed what they were feeling despite themselves: 'it was a lot to do with body language and the vocabulary used'.

There seems also to be have been a pattern to the comments inspectors have made when leaving the classroom. If they have felt comfortable with what they have seen, they have found it easier to show some appreciation and to express some warmth in their thanks. Conversely, when they have not liked what they have seen, they have been more likely to make a 'wordless departure' from the classroom. The accumulation of negative messages so undermined one teacher's confidence that 'he failed to arrive for the last day'. An inspector in this case felt that 'it was not fair to put so much extra pressure on such a vulnerable teacher, but what could we do?'

Although there may have been functional reasons for investing in relationships during an inspection, and explanations for the nature of those relationships, what seems to have mediated in the mechanistic process of inspection can ultimately only be described as human nature.

Earlier, I suggested that some democratic principle might be operating, whereby inspectors feel obliged to give teachers access to their work. Since there seems to be little evidence that inspectors have been given any particular ethical guidance of such a kind, we return again to the idea that people have operated according to their intuitions, schooled perhaps by the more basic principle of respect for persons (see Peters 1966).

The teachers in one case recounted how 'the key moment was when we had a conversation with the lead inspector. I thought, my God! he's human! It broke the ice.' In the same case, an inspector commented how 'people get closer to people as a result of the interviews. The team's credibility is challenged. It forces a more direct and personal involvement – seeing teachers as human beings. You start to look for more positives.'

These two accounts reveal the power of the interpersonal element in inspection. Once the human face had been revealed, the dynamic of the inspection seems to have changed. The after-school conversation between the teachers and the lead inspector had not been planned. It was a spontaneous part of the inspection which transformed the whole experience. Neither were interviews planned into inspection procedure to uncover the human dimension, but they have consistently demonstrated its existence.

Perhaps the unpredictability by which human nature has revealed itself in these two examples brings us closer to an understanding of how relationships might best be 'managed' in the context of inspection. Headteachers and teachers have placed considerable emphasis on the desirability of 'interpersonal skills' amongst inspectors; suggesting that 'inspectors manage morale' and that 'their credibility lies in handling people'. It has not been easy to discover exactly how this has been done. The secret may have lain in the simple acknowledgement by inspectors that the human dimension existed and was significant. Some inspectors have missed the point. In two of the cases where the lead inspector did take the trouble to brief the staff beforehand, any intention to establish positive relationships foundered on the hard persona the lead inspector presented. Similarly, inspectors' attempts to mix with the staff at coffee time were seen as 'insensitive'. Instead it has been the more subtle human touches which seem to have made the difference: the joke told to a group of children within the hearing of two teachers, a particular smile, the gentle acknowledgement on leaving a classroom.

So the lead inspector who explained that he understood the teachers' fears may well have been operating from a stronger motivation than a mere preference 'to engage in a human process'. Could it be that this human process lies at the heart of qualitative methodology? One inspector suggested that 'you can only operate as others allow'. This could be called into question. Another inspector claimed that she had worked in a situation where there had been 'powerful antagonism from the head and staff of the school' but that 'the antagonism did not distort our judgement'. Similarly, the one case where there were the greatest inconsistencies in procedure, the strongest tensions within the inspection team, and the worst relationships between the lead inspector and the staff, seems nevertheless to have produced a report which most of the teachers had regarded as 'fair'. But neither of these cases actually contradicts the basic assertion. In the case of the antagonistic school, we do not know whether the inspectors' judgements were accepted, either purely as judgements or for development. And, in the case where there was a disastrous process, if the teachers accepted the report as fair, it was because they allowed the inspectors to operate in that way. There were other teachers in that inspection, including those who most needed to accept the findings, who did not. They were able to displace the inspectors' findings.

Connection

The particular difficulties experienced by one lead inspector were compounded by her having had previous contact with the school: 'I'm not sure if I was the right person to lead it. I knew G— [the head]. I could have been compromised because of that. It would have been better done by someone who didn't know the school. Procedurally it is easier in a familiar school, but it is harder to deliver a hard message.'

There was some consternation amongst local authority inspectors and headteachers when the 1992 Education (Schools) Act ruled that Ofsted inspections could only be carried out by inspectors who had had no previous connection with the school. The case studies have spanned the period when people have had to adjust to this idea, although only three of the cases involved teams where there had been no previous connection by any member of the inspection team.

None of the inspectors has suggested that connection has made any difference to the objectivity of their judgements – the main argument behind the ruling – although it has affected some of the 'tailoring' of findings. But both inspectors and teachers have spoken of the significance of connection in relationships.

In general terms, both teachers and inspectors have seen connection as advantageous to the establishment of initial relationships: 'It makes life a little bit easier if you've met them before – easier to chat.' This comment has been echoed by teachers in three other cases but it was also contradicted: 'I'd rather not know the inspectors beforehand.'

At the same time, inspectors have tended toward the view that prior connection with the school could make the delivery of their findings more difficult, but there has been some ambivalence: 'It can get a bit close. If difficulties are going to have to be revealed it can be awkward – but the immediate adviser does bring useful background information.' But another inspector in this school added an important rider to this point of view: 'If there is a difficulty, you may need to be an outsider – it will be easier to say things straight – but – you may more easily be misunderstood.' A third inspector in this school put it this way: 'Whether the school got a better deal because the local man led the inspection I don't know. I just don't know if it was less fair or objective. But it must have had an effect.'

There were some difficulties to feedback in this case. The lead inspector appears to have been able to put his messages across to the headteacher. At the same time, there was a suggestion from this third inspector that the relationship between the lead inspector and the headteacher had been too close and that he had been too protective of the school. She felt that he had left out some findings which related more directly to the headteacher's effectiveness as a leader.

In other cases, an inspector felt that it was 'easier to feed back hard messages to people I know', and a headteacher expressed a clear preference for 'people I know – it is easier to take criticism and advice from someone you know'. The inspectors in this latter case did not agree with this headteacher. The lead inspector commented that 'there is a difficulty in inspecting your own patch' and one of his team felt that 'It wasn't always helpful that the lead inspector had had previous contact with the school.'

So what can we conclude about connection? Once again, the issue seems to revolve around whether the inspection has primarily a judgemental or developmental intent. It may have been easier to adopt a judgemental agenda where there has been no history of relationships. The inspectors could interpret the data with a fresh eye and if necessary feed back difficult findings. In only one case did an inspector feel that this would be helped by a previous relationship. On the other hand, it seems to have been easier, particularly for the school, to experience the inspection as a developmental event where there had been a previous history of relationships. Since the tone of Ofsted inspections has a distinctively judgemental flavour, it is unsurprising that the legal position for such inspections stipulates that there should be no previous connection.

Nevertheless, the issue seems to have been as much about preference as about the soundness of reported judgements. Although there was a suggestion in one case that the reported findings were distorted by the closeness of relationships, and in another the lead inspector clearly felt unsettled by prior connection, seven other cases involved inspectors who were known to the school. There was no suggestion in any of these that judgements had been impaired; difficult findings were certainly reported and fed back.

Gender

Just as there has been some discussion by both teachers and inspectors about connection, so have there been several references to gender. We have already seen how gender played its part in the dynamics of inspection teams. Teachers seem also to have been aware from time to time of the gender of particular inspectors though it has not always been clear how significant this has been. A comment such as 'I didn't like the science lady – she was officious' does not seem to do more than identify the inspector who focused on science as a woman. The adjective 'officious' can be applied to either sex.

On the other hand, a woman's comment such as this suggests greater significance: 'I may be being sexist, but the team were male while the lead inspector was a woman. There was an atmosphere. I was much more relaxed when she wasn't able to be there on the last day.' The headteacher in this school suggested that 'A male–female thing came into it – some of the women felt more comfortable with men.' There was a hint of this in another case where the female headteacher appeared to become overdependent on the male lead inspector. This was noticed by other members of the inspection team and the headteacher herself compared the male lead inspector with her usual local adviser – a woman – suggesting that he inspired 'greater confidence'.

A preference for men was not universal. In two cases, teachers commented that they could 'relate more to the woman'; 'women are not as harsh'. These comments were made by women.

Women did not feature among those who chose to comment on female inspectors as 'formidable'. One male headteacher described the only woman member of the inspection team as 'a strong-willed lady – quite outspoken – people have a reputation. She could run an assertiveness course for women quite easily.' In this inspection, all the inspectors were required by their procedures to ask teachers about equal opportunities. Several (male) teachers appeared to have assumed that this question had been prompted by the woman member of the inspection team.

This female inspector commented that it was particularly important to have a male–female balance in the inspection team for this school where both the head and deputy were male. She felt 'it was a patriarchal management team'. The same issue had surfaced in another case where both head and deputy were male. In this case there had been a particularly close relationship between the male lead inspector and the male headteacher. One of the female inspectors commented that 'I hope that there would be a recognition by the head and deputy that they could use the strengths of the staff more.' One of her female colleagues went further: 'The head is not developing the women staff. He didn't know that B— had aspirations for promotion. Women are undervalued in this county. Two of the women far surpassed the deputy in talent but had no official position.'

In both of these cases, the head and deputy were far outnumbered by women on the staff. In one of these cases, there was only one other man. In the other there were no other men.

The actual gender balance of the inspection teams in the 12 case studies was as Table 7.1:

Table 7.1

Case study	Men	Women	Lead inspector
1	1	2	male
2	3	1	female
3	3	2	male
4	2	3	male
5	4	3	female
6	1	2	female
7	2	1	male
8	4	1	female
9	3	1	male
10	2	2	male
11	3	1	male
12	3	1	male

Given the tendency of teachers to look for ways of displacing the validity of the inspection findings, it is perhaps unsurprising that gender was used as another way to differentiate the inspectors. Sometimes gender has been mentioned when it has not seemed to be the real issue. Despite the fact that the majority of primary teachers are women, there was no comment about the preponderance of men in inspection teams. The comment of a male HMI might help to point up a general issue about female inspectors: 'They are strong personalities who may have worked hard against male odds. Many primary school heads are men. There is a historical expectation that an HMI will be a man. My male colleagues seem generally to be more relaxed.'

Although some teachers were able to appreciate having a woman to relate to, there was some sense that the gender issue was there to be pounced on when an excuse was needed, and that women inspectors sometimes had to work harder to establish or to sustain their credentials.

Ritual

There was occasionally a sense that the procedures for inspection were following a ritual pattern. This sense has been underlined by a few inspectors suggesting that they needed to be inducted into the 'right way of doing things', although this suggestion also relates to the inspectors' notion of 'doing a good job' which will be discussed further later. It would appear that the remarkable standardisation of the procedures from one inspection to another has not only stemmed from a consensus about the sensible way to gather data and craft it into a set of corporate judgements. It has also provided inspectors with a ritual by which they can manage difficult emotions. Through ritual, individuals have been able to move in dangerous territory without hurting themselves.

Moore (1992: 227) suggests that ritual is a way of avoiding real relationships. He points out that rituals can take on a life of their own, 'separated from the intentions of the one performing the rite'. Whilst he is urging people to look for the deeper meaning which lies behind rituals, the force of his argument lies in his perception that there is a prevalence of 'empty ritual' which he equates to 'behaviour without feeling.' In the context of inspection, ritual seems to have been behaviour to mask feeling.

As with relationships, the manifestations of ritual have been rather one-sided. For the teachers, there have been hints of ritual in their preparations for the inspection, a time when they have needed the security of some kind of choreography to relieve or mask their high levels of anxiety. But the most ritualistic aspects of the process have been reserved for the moments when the inspectors seem to have felt the greatest anxiety. How should they enter the school on the first day? We saw earlier how one team filed in with their briefcases. This apparently spontaneous need to enter the school together in order to present a united front at a moment of considerable tension suggests that the presence of Black Rod would not have been out of place, ready to knock at the door. There has been similar ritual at the meeting where oral feedback is given to the headteacher. The lead inspector has gone through a standard explanation that 'our judgements cannot be challenged', ensuring that the headteacher and the deputy head are placed in the position of 'the accused' before a judge giving sentence. In this way, the inspectors have been able to handle the difficulty of conveying awkward messages.

Dress seems to have played a significant part in this. Male inspectors have admitted that they put on a suit for inspection. One inspector explained that 'I wear my smartest suit for feedback to the governors. If you are feeling good you can perform well.' This suggestion of 'performance' places the inspector in a role, just as a priest would wear special clothes to officiate at eucharist. In one case, the teachers were quite disconcerted by the difference in the demeanour and dress of an inspector who had worn a sweater when leading a course but who now wore his suit. He claimed that 'I don't consciously behave differently on inspections – but that may not be how others see me.' One lead inspector described how a colleague had deliberately 'dressed down' for an inspection. He had wanted to break through the ritual but had finished up 'being rather out of place – it didn't really come off'.

Echoing the earlier references to gender, women inspectors have also considered carefully what they are going to wear. One commented: 'I used to power dress – why do I need to do that? My insecurity? Telling the teachers that I'm working differently? I normally wear a suit on feedback day – my own emotional state. HMI women definitely power dress – for sure.' Another suggested that 'It's easier to be nasty if you're formally dressed.'

This reference to formality echoes comments made by teachers in another case who were 'surprised that the team was less approachable than we expected'. One of them commented that he'd 'expected more "friendly" relationships though I can see in retrospect that it was correct'. Again, the impression is given of people in role, playing appropriate parts which insulate them from the emotions their messages might arouse.

Bernstein, Elvin and Peters (1966: 432), writing about rituals in schools, suggest that: 'The symbolic function of ritual is to relate the individual through ritualistic acts to a social order, to heighten respect for that order, to revivify that order within the individual and, in particular, to deepen acceptance of the procedures used to maintain continuity, order and boundary and which control ambivalence towards the social order.'

They suggest that rituals help to 'construct a framework of meaning' and that they 'also serve to prevent questioning of the values and social order' (p. 432). They cite ritual as 'a form of restricted code', suggesting that 'the major meanings in ritual are extra-verbal or indirect; for they are not made verbally explicit. Ritual is a form of restricted code' (p. 434).

In the context of school rituals, they suggest that there is a 'controlling sentiment', citing 'shame' and 'guilt'. In inspection, the controlling sentiment seems to have been anxiety. It is not difficult to recognise the parallels between the ritualistic characteristics of inspection and those which Bernstein *et al.* identified in the way that schools maintain a social order. The case of inspection does differ in respect of the idea of continuity. In inspection, there is no need for inspectors to retain control beyond the duration of the inspection itself. However, continuity does need to exist, since the inspectors do not have time to negotiate any social order before they arrive. Continuity seems to lie in the mythology of inspection.

Bernstein *et al.* raised another issue which has its parallel in inspection. They suggested that as pupils become more individually differentiated in schools there is a shift from 'stratified', 'bureaucratic' control towards interpersonal 'therapeutic' control. This shift seems to reflect the differences between the judgemental and developmental modes of inspection. The ritualistic elements of inspection seem to have been strongest when the inspectors have needed to assert their position as examiners or judges at the outset and when they have delivered their results or verdicts at the end. In the meanwhile, they have been able to break through the formality of their roles and functions, apparently desiring to respond to the human feelings in the situation and to secure ownership of their ideas and findings. Even when they have done this, they appear to have succeeded in maintaining control.

I have treated the ritualistic elements of inspection primarily in the context of the management of feelings: inspections have generated strong feelings which ritual has helped to control or contain. Bernstein *et al.*'s consideration of ritual focused on a more political context. Inspection's ritual elements certainly have their place in the larger, political, context of the changed culture of inspection, particularly subsequent to the 1992 Education (Schools) Act. The published report of an Ofsted or HMI inspection is intended to contribute to the market forces by which schools will survive or fail. Ultimately, the relationships which pertain in such an inspection are subject to this political reality.

The scapegoats of inspections

Although there have been suggestions of ritual sacrifice in the way that inspectors and teachers have described inspection – an Abraham of inspectors leading an Isaac of teachers to the sacrificial altar – there has been a more persistent incidence of scapegoats than of sacrificial lambs in the 12 case studies. In every single case, the inspectors seem to have identified one or two teachers who have come in for their continual criticism. Such criticism seems sometimes to have become exaggerated, as if the inspectors have needed a negative 'foil' against which to make positive comparisons. We have already seen how inspectors can find themselves being caught in 'a negative hole'. Although they have usually managed to find positive things to redress the balance in the report as a whole, this does not seem to have exonerated particular individuals. In perhaps the most extreme case, 'people used nicknames – "Stormin' Norman" – that guy became a caricature – he was the worst teacher – he wasn't the only weak teacher but he became the dustbin.'

It has not been easy to find an explanation for this negative stereotyping by the inspectors. It may have been the particular challenge that such teachers placed on the balance of the inspection findings: 'We had this concern over a particular blip – we didn't want to hit them over the head or let them miss its significance.' Or it may have been a reflection of the slight sense of embarrassment which inspectors seem to have felt when confronted by bad practice. One inspector talked with particular feeling about her discomfort at putting pressure on a vulnerable teacher. But this does not explain the identification of at least one particular weak teacher in every single case, even cases where the school as a whole received a positive report. One inspector talked of 'two teachers who caught the negative'. This is similar to the idea of the 'dustbin'. Perhaps we have to conclude that the inspectors needed a scapegoat, or that, when put under pressure, the structure broke at its weakest point, or perhaps we can only conclude that there was at least one teacher in each case where the inspectors, despite their best intentions, were unable to find sufficient evidence to say that his or her performance was 'satisfactory'.

Unfortunately, despite the fact that the inspections set out to report on schools as whole institutions, the identity of the weakest teachers has always been revealed, at least to the headteacher. These teachers featured strongly in the 'unofficial' feedback to the headteacher and could often be found in the report, at least by those inside the school: 'We have looked at the report and areas of weakness – we can pinpoint members of staff. Such people have an effect on the whole report. I haven't seen those people recognising they should do something about it. We are going to have to grasp the nettle.'

The identification of individuals has had a variety of consequences. Curiously, although headteachers have recognised in several cases that they may have nettles to grasp, and one head commented that 'you are only as strong as your weakest person', there has been little sense of the teachers looking for a scapegoat. Solidarity has been their more general reaction; they have stood by one another, even when they have seen criticism as justified. Indeed, the headteachers themselves seem to have looked to protect the staff rather than to take them on. One headteacher had not shared the report with anyone except his deputy. He pointed out that 'you cannot have anonymity in small schools'. Another headteacher optimistically assumed that the teachers 'would have picked up criticisms in the report', although they did not seem to have done so.

In as many as five cases, the teachers who had been identified to the headteacher as unsatisfactory did not appear to know of this, even though, in all of these cases, some weeks had elapsed since the inspection and the report had been received by the school. In all of these cases, at least one person other than the headteacher did know.

It may not then be surprising that a significant consequence of the identification of a negative performer by the inspectors has been either physical or psychological breakdown. If teachers have suspected that things have gone wrong but have not been told, this would place considerable pressure on them. If, alternatively, it has been made clear that their practice has been found to be inadequate, there would also be stress. In five separate cases, at least one teacher has had a prolonged absence immediately after the inspection. In one of these cases, there was no suggestion that the teacher concerned had not performed satisfactorily. Nevertheless, there was a general consensus that the heart attack she had immediately after the inspection was, at least in part, brought on by it. In the other four cases, it was one of the teachers who had been criticised who went absent. Two of these had not lasted the length of the inspection itself.

The fact that, at the end of the day, the inspections have identified particular individuals must be a significant factor in teachers' strongly personalised perceptions of inspection. As one teacher commented, 'This teacher was heavily criticised unofficially by the lead inspector to the head. It's not just an inspection of the school, it is the teachers.' This is borne out by the experience of two teachers who, as a direct result of an inspection, found themselves faced with formal procedures for incompetence. Such negative experiences must also contribute powerfully to the mythology of inspection.

The experience of one particular teacher would have certainly made a permanent impact on her colleagues. In this inspection, the inspectors had identified two teachers, both senior and long-serving in the school, as having particularly poor practice. Another teacher in the school had somehow picked up that 'these particular weak teachers had dominated the oral feedback to the head'. The head related how the lead inspector had suggested that for one of them the only answer was to 'sack her', and another inspector had described this same teacher as 'past her sell-by date'. This teacher had felt that she had been identified negatively in the inspection report. At the staff meeting where the lead inspector had fed back the inspection findings, she raised a query about this. As a colleague described, the lead inspector 'kept saying "can't change it" – when R— queried it, the inspector said "tough". This was seen as the last straw for R—'. She had not been in school since.

In the sample covered by this research, this particular inspection has consistently provided the worst-case scenario as far as relationships have been concerned. Nevertheless, it is perhaps significant that the only example of such public humiliation has been at the hands of an inspector. Given the stress which whole institutions have been under – at least three cases have had particularly negative reports – it may seem a little surprising that the teachers themselves have not turned on one of their colleagues, even though they have talked privately of the need to do something to rectify the problem. Instead they have offered mutual support. Staff solidarity, far from being undermined, seems to have been strengthened. At the same time, there has repeatedly been the sense that many teachers have lived in anticipation of being a casualty. In the relief of being able to say 'there but for the grace of God go I', teachers have given their less fortunate colleagues space to lick their wounds. There may have been scapegoats for inspectors; but not, at least publicly, for the teachers. For them, their apparent passivity in the face of inspection has created more of a sense of being the victims of fate or the casualties of fortune than being the scapegoats of ritual.

8 OUTCOMES OF

INSPECTION

This chapter outlines what the participants of inspections thought the outcomes of inspection had been, or were likely to be. These are considered in five sections: the judgemental outcomes of the reports themselves; the validation the inspections provided; instrumental formative outcomes; conceptual formative outcomes; and the inspectors' views about likely outcomes.

When first formulating the research questions, I did not appreciate how much a school might be affected by an inspection while it was happening. I had an expectation that inspection would make a longer-term impact and that it would be not be too difficult to find a causal relationship between things that happened during an inspection and subsequent changes or actions.

It did not take very long before I began to be disabused of my initial expectations and assumptions. By embarking on a project which asked people to voice their perceptions and feelings, it quickly became clear that simple cause–effect relationships would rarely emerge and that my qualitative judgements would not be equivalent to proof. The tension between a positivist, quasi-scientific, and a qualitative view of inspection became all too apparent.

The relationships between expectations and intentions, behaviour and emotions, and subsequent action and learning must somehow be brought together. We are in something of a quandry. The positivist view of inspection cannot be ignored. Although inspection uses an essentially qualitative methodology, the cultures of managerialism and market accountability, combined with a

clear expectation that inspection will somehow be 'formative' have prompted several teachers and headteachers to identify direct, apparently mechanistic, effects from their inspections.

Although this may be the case, I would suggest that these teachers and headteachers may themselves be caught up in a positivist view and are giving themselves too little credit for such, allegedly direct, outcomes. Henkel (1991) asserts that the positivist view is inappropriate since it places the school in a passive position – with inspection in the driving seat – whereas the school drives itself. Changes may have occurred when the teacher or headteacher have been convinced of the need for the change. But it has been their change; neither the inspection nor the inspectors have actually effected it – the inspectors have left the scene.

However, there has also been a set of more indirect outcomes. Teachers and headteachers have speculated about whether the inspection will or will not have made a difference. They have suggested that some things were more likely to occur than they might have been and, in particular, they have talked about things happening sooner rather than later – whilst often claiming that they would have happened eventually even if the inspection had not occurred. But the most substantial subset of this kind of indirect outcome has related to insight and reflection. The inspection has made people think. This accords with Coleman and Larocque's (1990) suggestion that data from assessment can be used both 'instrumentally for direct action and conceptually for insight'. Whether conceptual insight will lead to future action, and whether that future action could be attributed to the inspection, are open to question. However, I would suggest that these are likely, in the longer term, to be among the more substantial and significant outcomes of the inspections. I shall attempt to support this position in the next chapter with evidence and argument; though I may persuade, I shall still be a long way short of proof.

Judgemental outcomes

A legitimate report

The use of the word 'effect' tends to hold us on the developmental side of the judgement–development divide. The word 'outcome' can include developmental effects without excluding the judgemental outcomes. Apart from one case, all of the inspections have generated a report. Even this case provided an account for the inspectors' future reference: 'We achieved the agenda. We confirmed that we are happy to answer anything about the school.'

This latter example shows that much of the significance of inspection might be missed if we look straight away for developmental outcomes. Ironically, this inspection changed from a check on the school's National Curriculum assessment procedures to a developmental agenda almost before it started; the teachers were trying out the inspectors' suggestions while the inspection was still in process. But these LEA inspectors set out with the intention of pre-empting an HMI inspection; the outcome was that they satisfied themselves that all was well. In one sense, any developmental outcomes, of which there were several, were unofficial. The official developmental outcomes would have come had the school not satisfied the inspectors. Matters would have had to be put right or heads might have rolled.

Another case study had a similar agenda. The LEA sent in the inspectors because there were concerns about the school's management. The inspectors were able to publish a report, internally to the LEA, which said that there was no cause for concern. The report did also contain recommendations which were acted upon, but it was the bill of health which mattered – to the LEA and to the school.

We need to be confident that the account of a school's strengths and weaknesses produced by the inspectors was valid as a judgemental outcome. If the inspectors produced a report which was not worth the paper it was written on, that would not have been the same outcome as one which provided a secure, comprehensive, reliable and valid account of the school's strengths and weaknesses.

I have not been in a position to decide whether the inspection reports presented valid accounts of what was taking place within the school. I have been able to look at the comprehensiveness of the range of headings covered by the reports and to make an assessment as to whether the tone of the report matched the inspectors' expressed intentions in the context of the judgement–development polarity. For example, one report contained few explicit judgements about standards. The emphasis was on the teaching provision, as opposed to the learning outcomes, and its collection of recommendations showed that it was intended more as a developmental document than as a judgemental one.

In any assessment of an inspection report as a judgemental document it is the perception of the intended audiences which matters. In the research interviews, inspectors, headteachers and teachers identified a number of stakeholders in inspection. It is beyond the scope of this book to ascertain the extent to which the accounts offered by these case studies were seen as legitimate or significant by many of these stakeholders. If the government, LEA, governors or parents had acted at school level as a result of reading an account which they found legitimate, then it is likely that the school would have commented. But we do not know what contribution these single reports will have made to the accumulation of data at the wider systems level.

Coleman and Larocque (1990) found little direct evidence in their study of a district-wide evaluation system in Canada of any significant subsequent action by the district at school level. They did suggest that the accumulation of data had affected decision-making in relation to the allocation of resources, particularly for development. Lawton (1988) was sceptical of the impact on government of the digest of HMI activity incorporated in the Chief Inspector's annual report. He made no suggestion of external action at the level of the school following an individual inspection. But Henkel (1991) argued that this is a mistaken expectation of inspection anyway. She saw the process of inspection as a means of imposing a political ideology rather than as a direct lever for action. This would place inspection into a more formative domain, where the implicit or explicit criteria of the inspection contribute to an evolving picture of what the 'professional' should be doing. One inspector mentioned that he saw little response on the part of his LEA to inspection reports. He seemed to be assuming that it was up to the inspection and advisory service to follow up issues raised. This would require the assent of those within the school.

No headteacher or teacher in any of the case studies has referred to any externally imposed consequence following their inspection. We cannot conclude from this that the government or the LEA have seen any lack of legitimacy in the inspection reports, only that they do not seem to have acted. However, the negative mythology of inspection may well have been significant in this context. Two headteachers in particular were uncomfortably aware that a 'poor' inspection report would leave them in a vulnerable position. Similarly, two other headteachers were under particular scrutiny. Had they not passed muster, they too would have felt vulnerable.

But what was this vulnerability? We have seen how there has been a particular victim, or 'scapegoat', in every inspection. Some of these teachers have had periods of extended absence as a result of the 'stress' of the inspection. It is possible, perhaps probable, that this absence would have led quite quickly to a 'resignation' on the grounds of ill health. We do know of two teachers who were faced with formal procedures for incompetence following, ironically, one of the most 'advisory' of the case studies. Besides these teachers who have already succumbed to the stress of the inspection, there was another group who may have found themselves under stress following the inspection. These were the teachers whom heads have been prompted, more often through 'unofficial' feedback, to 'take on':

'It will enable me to do things with B—.'

'The inspection has reawakened the need to ensure that those children in G—'s class get a fairer deal.'

'They told me who I needed to take on.'

'The inspection will force this teacher to face up to the National Curriculum requirements.'

The judgemental account provided by the inspectors seems to have provided a direct impetus for headteachers to tackle issues of competence. None of the headteachers has questioned the validity of the inspectors' adjudication of these teachers' performance. However, it is difficult to decide whether this is, or is not, a true example of external accountability. These teachers were not identified in any written report. Indeed, they could not be, since the inspection was an institutional review; individual teachers would not be named in the report. The responsibility for the competence of teachers is internal to the school and its governors. The inspectors' contribution to the situation was predominantly to offer a credible professional opinion. This is demonstrated by the fact that both HMI, who are not LEA personnel, and LEA inspectors have prompted headteachers to act. At the same time, however, the practice of these teachers has contributed to the overall assessment of the quality of the school's teaching. This sense of being only as strong as the weakest part is likely to have added to the pressure on the headteacher to act.

That verdicts on the professional competence of individual teachers have been outcomes of inspections underlines the strong sense of personalisation described by many teachers facing inspection. One aspect of this was promotion. There has been little direct evidence of professional advancement following these cases. However, two teachers were promoted very soon after their inspection. A direct link cannot be identified, but two of the inspectors were subsequently involved in the selection processes for these promotions. Another teacher was explicitly told that she should seek promotion. One teacher also identified that one of the inspectors had 'arranged for me to go on a course'. The course in question was a prestigious one, not for the incompetent.

Teachers were vulnerable because adverse inspection findings could make their position intolerable. This is strictly a professional issue; the teacher would reach the conclusion that he or she could not perform according to a consensus of professional expectation. The vulnerability of the headteacher would have been the same, except that it would be for someone else to sustain the pressure following an inspection. The comments of some inspectors about follow-up suggest that they might be the agents of such pressure, both as representatives of the LEA and as senior professionals. The governors could also have a role in this. Since none of the cases researched pointed to any serious dereliction by a headteacher, we have no evidence to show how governors might have acted.

As we have seen, governors seem to have placed themselves outside the inspections I have researched. Nevertheless they have always been an audience to the report. Had there been any questioning of the legitimacy of the inspectors' findings, it is likely that it would have surfaced in my data.

One of the expectations of the inspection process has been that the school should draw up an action plan to address the issues raised by the inspectors. Under the Ofsted procedures this was, strictly speaking, the responsibility of the governors. In all of these cases, the governors seemed to assume that the headteacher would present an action plan for their approval. An action plan had been, or was in the process of being, drawn up by the headteacher, either alone or with the senior management team, in every case except one. Although the action plan would be a developmental outcome of inspection, its existence may help to explain how the accountability offered by inspection has worked in relation to these external audiences.

Government, LEA and governors have not normally been expected to take direct action as a result of an individual inspection. This situation has changed since provisions for schools in need of 'special measures' have been implemented under the Ofsted procedures. However, for schools outside this net, the consequences of inspection remain unclear. The disciplining of a headteacher might be unnecessary if the inspection report itself 'forced' a resignation. The general expectation would be that the school would respond to an inspection with an action plan and that LEA inspectors would be available for follow-up. Provided that the school accepts the findings of the inspectors as legitimate and does not cry 'foul', then it is sufficient that inspections are 'seen to be done'. The reporting by the inspectors to governors would then ensure this visibility.

The proviso of legitimacy is important for it links inextricably the processes of inspection with the outcome of the report. We have seen how teachers and headteachers have looked to displace the legitimacy of the inspectors' findings, on grounds of procedure, credibility or relationship. Although, ironically, the teachers who most needed to accept the findings of inspectors seem often to have been fiercest in their rejection of them, there has been no outright rejection of the 'fairness' of a report sufficient to undermine its acceptance by external parties. We could speculate that one or two headteachers might have been able to undermine the current relevance of the report to the school's developmental priorities, but even in these cases, the professional legitimacy of the report has seemed secure.

Does this explanation of how the accountability function of inspection might work (above the line of 'special measures') for the 'contractual' agencies of the LEA and governors and for the 'political' agency of government also work for the market accountability to parents? There were only two case studies in which the report was circulated to parents. I have not explored parents' views of the legitimacy or significance of inspection. However, in a market sense, we might expect there to have been some impact on the school's enrolment. The research interviews took place too soon after these two inspections for there to be any evidence that parents might have removed their children from the school or failed to enrol new children as a result of the inspection. Nevertheless, the issue of parental confidence in the school was certainly seen as significant by headteachers. Almost all of them made references to this, and two of them in particular had made the most of the inspectors' positive findings in their parent newsletters. They were following the idea of market accountability by using the inspection to 'market' their schools.

Validation

The messages used by these headteachers in their newsletters to parents were the positive messages. If inspection is seen as a tool for accountability, it will not be surprising to discover that headteachers and teachers have valued these positive messages:

'It validated our practice.'

'It gave official sanction for all sorts of things.'

'The inspection gave J— and me a pat on the back.'

'They did pick out positives – it had a beneficial effect on people's morale.'

'It underlined what we're good at – that gives us confidence.'

'We felt vindicated – our achievements were acknowledged – we felt they really recognised the ethos and dedication.'

'It supported our direction – it was a validation.'

'I felt more valued.'

'A number of things were confirmed.'

'It confirmed what we knew needed to be done.'

'We had worked hard on pupil management and it came out well – a pat on the back encourages future effort.'

'It was a confirmation.'

It is again difficult to separate judgement from development in these comments. 'Validation' and 'confirmation' are rubber-stamp words. They signify approval. However, there was a strong sense that it was not a static picture that was being approved. Even when the inspectors were validating what was happening at the time, there was a simultaneous appraisal of the school's developmental direction. If the inspectors did not make a recommendation because they saw the school's own developmental agenda positively, presumably we should interpret this non-intervention as a developmental outcome. The effect of voicing approval brings us back to the interrelationship between action and emotion which we found within the process of inspection. When the school's performance has been validated, teachers' motivation and confidence have been enhanced.

The relationship between judgement and development which emerges from the case studies is less a polarity and more a sequence. Judgement seems to have preceded development in two respects. Firstly, it was in the judgemental mode that judgements were made about the strengths and weaknesses of the school. Subsequently, these judgements provided the bases for developmental diagnosis, making it possible for inspectors to raise 'key issues' and make recommendations. When teachers have been anxious about judgement, particularly those who have been less confident about their practice, they have resisted it outright, which we have seen repeatedly (firstly in Chapter 4). This seems to have obscured their understanding that appropriate developmental suggestions need to be based on a proper judgemental understanding of what needs to be done. Such teachers have perhaps had a view of the inspector as expert which has led them to expect off-the-peg advice, as opposed to bespoke suggestions, matched to assessed need.

The tendency of less confident teachers to be more anxious about judgement points to the second sequential relationship between judgement and development. The confirmation and validation offered by the validation of judgement seems to have given teachers confidence. Confidence seems to have been a prerequisite for professional reflection. Thus, again, the situation has both technical and emotional dimensions, as has the process of inspection itself. The judgements have provided the technical data on which to build developmental action; they have also provided the validating confidence which has underpinned developmental motivation and reflection. Thus a headteacher could say of inspection: 'It was a personal shot in the arm to take the next step.'

Confidence alone may not be sufficient to provide a link between judgement and development. It may be that the reflective practitioner is one who has developed a cognitive understanding of what judgement entails and recognises it as a prerequisite to development. I shall explore this further in the next chapter.

To summarise: the judgemental outcome of each case study has been an account which seems to have been generally accepted as legitimate. The inspection itself, as an event, completed by its account and the associated action plan, seems to have provided the necessary 'visible' evidence to outside agencies that 'quality' is being managed. Where the legitimate account has validated practice in the school, this has generated confidence and motivation. Judgement should be viewed sequentially with development, technically, emotionally and, perhaps, cognitively.

Instrumental formative outcomes

As was suggested at the start of this chapter, headteachers and teachers have seen some of the outcomes of inspection as being the direct result of inspection. This fits Coleman and Larocque's (1990) idea of the 'instrumental' use of inspection findings for 'direct action'. While we were exploring the processes of inspection, there were several aspects of inspection itself which immediately made a change. In different ways and in different cases, all of these changes became more permanent.

Inspection requires schools to submit documents for scrutiny. We have seen how some schools did not have all the documents that were required. In one of these, there was extensive document writing immediately prior to the inspection, and in another, the headteacher conceded the value of a written policy framework, even though he had resisted it prior to inspection. Other headteachers admitted that 'the review prompted an audit of the school's curriculum documentation' or, referring to policy-writing, that the inspection 'brings things forward'. By using the documentation as a reference point for their judgements, particularly in the context of curriculum planning, the inspectors seem to have demonstrated their value. The policies and plans which were drafted for the inspection remained in existence afterwards and there was a new acknowledgement of a need for other documents.

We have also seen how the inspectors asked that teachers have copies of their short-term planning available for scrutiny. Again, teachers seem to have recognised the extra control this gave them over the quality of their classroom practice and some continued with a practice that they had initiated specifically for the inspection.

The way inspectors asked individual teachers to speak on behalf of their colleagues about subjects or aspects of the curriculum seems to have had a direct impact on schools' interpretation of the role of subject coordinators. One head commented, following the inspection: 'I shall be expecting more from the coordinators.' In one or two schools, it looked as if this might also have had an effect on the way that the curriculum is conceived: 'we have looked again at our curriculum map'; and 'I have become much more aware of how individual subjects are or are not covered'.

In addition to these requirements of the process of inspection, an awareness of what the inspectors were looking for seems to have prompted direct action by teachers on such things as differentiation, curriculum planning and classroom practice: 'I'm more aware of classroom procedures and different ways of teaching.' In a few cases, inspectors made suggestions. In one, an inspector made an inappropriate and unhelpful suggestion, about obtaining cushions for reading corners, which was dismissed by the teachers and served only to undermine the inspector's credibility. In another, a teacher pointed out, rather sarcastically, that 'we now have an indoor portable waterplay'. The underlying message was clear: she had been asked about water play and had done something about it, but she was not convinced. This seemed to be a classic case of 'strategic compliance' (Alexander 1991). In another case, the school had immediately changed their interpretation of the LEA's curriculum guidance to match what they thought the inspectors had wanted. This appeared to have been done in an unreflective, reactive way. The teacher who explained the change did not appear to understand what was now expected of her. We saw earlier how in one case a teacher's special performance for the inspectors had been so strongly validated that he had sustained the performance subsequently.

The danger of teachers acting immediately, without either ownership or reflection, on inspectors' suggestions seems to support the withholding of direct advice. A teacher recounted how 'we tried to do what they suggested but it didn't work' Nevertheless there has often been a temptation to act quickly on the inspectors' recommendations. One teacher proudly claimed that 'we've already done 90 per cent of the things they recommended'. But a lead inspector emphasised that 'we want them to go beyond the eight out of ten recommendations done, ticking-off approach. We want to come alongside a reflective process.'

Conceptual formative outcomes

Coleman and Laroque's other category of formative outcome is the conceptual outcome. Many teachers have expressed the view succinctly summed up by one: 'it made me think'. Several teachers have talked of the idea of the external observer:

'I found myself looking at my classroom as if I were a stranger.'

'You try to look at it through their eyes.'

'It makes you extra-critical of yourself – looking at yourself teaching.'

For others, the inspection 'concentrated our minds'; 'gave us a little push'; 'keeps you on your toes'; or 'sharpens you'.

However, all of these comments, and several others like them were more concerned with the periods before and during the inspection than afterwards.

Although they suggest a reflective response, it would be inappropriate to attribute significant depth of thought to all of them. For example, when a teacher said: 'I thought very carefully about what I would be doing while they were here', it was clear in the context of the research interview that this teacher was expressing more of an instinct for survival than significant conceptual insight.

Nevertheless, the inspection did promote thought and reflection, at whatever depth. There were other comments which suggested that this might have outlived the inspection itself:

'Since the report we have been looking carefully at what they said.'

'It has made me look carefully at my role and to justify it.'

'We've tightened up on things.'

'It has helped us to focus.'

'I got a clarification of issues.'

'Everybody is now stimulated – we don't want to get caught with our pants down again.'

For two schools, the process of the inspection was extended by their having conducted their own pre-inspection evaluation of the school. In both cases, this appears to have helped them to accept and take ownership of the inspectors' findings: 'We had done a Grids [self-evaluation] exercise so we knew our areas of weakness. Without exception, those were the areas pinpointed – there was a complete match.'

In one other case, despite some rather dismissive attitudes to the inspection, there had clearly been quite a lot of discussion. Afterwards, two teachers felt that the most valuable part of the inspection had been 'before the inspectors actually came'. It was not clear in either of these cases how long-lasting were the insights gained from the self-evaluation which the inspection had prompted. There would be a qualitative difference between self-evaluation which was focused on a 'best performance' during the inspection – probably to secure a positive judgemental verdict – and self-evaluation which enhanced the likelihood that any formative outcomes generated by the inspection would endure over time.

It must be said that if we were seeking to assess the outcomes of inspection by the volume of claims about developmental outcomes made by teachers and headteachers we would have to conclude that inspection was, overall, an expensive waste of time and money. This would particularly be the case if we gave too much weight to the several teachers' comments which suggested that the inspection had had little or no longer-term effect:

'I do not feel that the review has made much impact on me or my practice.'

'I don't think it will make us move any more quickly.'

'It had no effect on my practice.'

'There was a big build-up. It came and went. Now no one thinks about it.'

'I don't see that the inspection will have done much to change the school's development.'

'It reinforced one's cynicism that these people come and go at great expense and nothing really happens afterwards.'

'It blew over very quickly. I'd forgotten it shortly afterwards.'

'I wish it had been more developmental.'

'The inspection accelerated development – but we'd have got to the same point without it.'

However, these dismissive points were only matched by the headteacher in one case, the same case which generated three of the comments quoted above. This headteacher's view was that 'the inspection did not change anything', that it was 'something one goes through and out the other side' and that 'the staff have brushed it aside, marginalised it. It has become an isolated event.' Little wonder that the teachers said what they did. We have seen earlier that the problem with this inspection was that it took place more for the inspectors than for the school and was seen by them as an inconvenience. We shall see below that, although it was out of step with the pattern of headteachers, it did contribute significantly to the inspectors' own development.

We have to take the other dismissive comments at face value. At the same time, it may be worth pointing out that one headteacher presented a substantial list of formative effects of the inspection, including a 'fundamental change in the head-deputy partnership'. He felt that the inspection had had 'a significant impact on whole-school management', suggesting that whole-school reviews would be more likely to affect management than classroom practice. This reflects the balance of inspectors' opinion that the headteacher was ultimately the principal audience for their reporting and hence for the inspection itself.

Out of the 11 headteachers interviewed for this research, eight of them have been unequivocal about the benefits to their schools of inspection, despite the fact that two of them had had to accept quite substantial criticism of their management. Two of the remaining three were generally positive but had significant reservations. The remaining headteacher succeeded in undermining the inspection, perhaps ultimately because he found the inspectors' findings too unpalatable. Even he conceded that the inspection had 'helped to channel our planning in the senior management team' and accepted, albeit reluctantly, that he had teachers whom he needed to take on.

The benefit seen by the majority of the headteachers was that they could use the report 'as a tool' for development. 'It will support the professional development of the staff and the school in a formative way.' One head explained how it had 'revamped me – it picks out the inadequacies of your role. I shall pick up the pace. The greatest impact will be on my management – I shall tighten up the inspector-in-residence role.' This last point was echoed by another headteacher who felt that 'The need to monitor has been the biggest thing to come out of it.'

One reason why the volume of teachers' comments should not be taken as a guide to the developmental strength of the case studies lies in the timing of the case study interviews. It has not proved possible to conduct a set of follow-up interviews. Even if it had, it would have been difficult to disentangle the developmental impetus of inspection from other developments in the world of education even after 15 months. National Curriculum implementation had a continuing impact on schools throughout the research period and, for the second half of that time, the publication of the *Framework for the Inspection of Schools* (Ofsted 1992) generated extensive self-inspection and many 'pre-Ofsted audits', commissioned by schools, which diluted the effects of individual inspections. In the event, most of the case studies were conducted within weeks of the inspections themselves. This means that the questions about outcomes could often only outline what was likely to occur – a matter of perception. As we saw at the beginning of this chapter, the outcomes of inspection are the result of an interaction between inspectors and the school. The effects may not emerge for some time as the message percolates through the school's collective consciousness. As Biott and Nias (1992) comment, change at the level of belief or assumption needs pain and time. We may have seen the pain, but we may have needed to allow more time.

It has been possible to conduct a follow-up interview with one headteacher. Immediately after the inspection, he identified that the inspection had given the school a development plan. A year later, he confirmed that almost every issue that had been addressed developmentally by the school had originated from the inspection report. He saw the agenda from the inspection 'lasting for five years' and commented that 'the inspection was probably the most significant contributor to my development as a manager of my whole career'.

This headteacher also felt that the inspection had 'affected my relationship with the governors' for the better. We have seen how increased solidarity within the staff has been an outcome of inspection. A closer relationship between headteacher and governors was an additional outcome for several other headteachers. In two of these cases this seems also to have applied to the relationship between teachers and governors. These improvements in the relationship with governors are curious, given the governors' apparent lack of involvement in the inspections. A possible explanation lies in the fact that the governors have been a key audience to the report and have generally received oral feedback from the inspectors.

The governors' enhanced understanding of what takes place in the school may have made easier the communication between them and the staff. The inspections often seem to have been catalysts to headteachers' and teachers' recognition of their wider accountabilities. Since the governors represent a first line of accountability, perhaps the inspections have been an added incentive for governor-staff communication.

The inspectors' perspective

The inspectors have taken a more optimistic view of the formative outcomes of the inspections. Their aspirations were that inspection would lead to development. As ex-teachers, and ex-headteachers, mostly with an advisory background, they seem to have placed less emphasis on the judgemental outcomes of contractual or market accountability, except as a means to a more formative end. However, their expectations might have been tempered by their need to justify their existence. They have usually seen inspection in the context of a process of supported development which includes substantial follow-up. Despite an emerging breakdown in the traditional relationship between schools and a paternalistic LEA, at least some of the inspections would have provided the inspectors with an agenda which they would have expected to be active in carrying out. This loss of LEA influence was underlined by the fact that in two of the cases researched the schools subsequently became grant-maintained.

The particular focus for the inspectors was the headteacher. Inspectors in several cases have said that 'it will have been helpful for the head – it has given him bullets to fire'. The inspectors have seen themselves providing the headteacher with a report which contains an 'objective second opinion' that 'provides the head with a distancing process'. However, the inspectors could not know whether their work would have been formative, they could only hope: 'you hope that maybe you've moved the school forward'; or 'I'd see development as likely'.

The inspectors' faith that something developmental would come out of their work seems to have been based on an expectation that the school would use their findings reflectively:

'It may help the staff to think more deeply about their policy for learning – they had not really thought through the fundamentals it contained.'

'The visit will have helped them to review what they were doing and to see points to go forward and improve their practice.'

'The school will have had a closer look at itself because of it.'

But there was a strong sense that schools would need follow-up support if the inspection's formative potential was going to be fully realised. Inspectors made specific references to their expectations of follow-up in almost every case. One of these saw the inspection event and the follow-up as being quite separate: 'The action plan is implicit – development is the key purpose. But inspection is political – it's about accountability. It will be up to the people who follow the inspection to make it formative. I wouldn't anticipate that the school will be able to manage its own action plan.'

In one inspection, the inspectors were quite open about their purposes: 'the first purpose was the team's development'. It appears that the school felt in the end that the inspectors' 'team development' was at their expense. It does seem, up to a point, to have served the inspectors' purpose: 'It gave us a view of how to go about such reviews in the future.' At the same time, some of these inspectors recognised that they had not worked all that well as a team. They had presented separate sections in the report, had worked rather separately, and emerged with separate perceptions: 'it gave me access to my subject in the school'. This inspection was different from all of the others in the extent to which it seemed to have been as much for the inspectors as for the school. However, several commentators (e.g. Stillman and Grant 1989) have suggested that team inspection prior to 1988 had often placed a priority on the inspectors' development over the school's. This case seems to have reflected that previous culture.

Nevertheless, although these inspectors were openly working for themselves – whilst still working for the school – they have not been alone in this. The assumption that inspection would require follow-up seems to have put several inspectors close to a position where they were enduring inspection in the knowledge that they were generating the advisory work which most of them preferred. This is not to question the motives of the inspectors. We have seen how they have been fully committed to 'development' and a 'fair deal' for children. But, as the next chapter shows, it has been significant that their evaluation of inspections has focused at least as much on how well they think they performed as inspectors as it has on the potential developmental impact of what they have done.

9   PROFESSIONALISM

AND INSPECTION

This chapter will argue that professionalism and inspection
are inextricably intertwined. It will show how professionalism
embraces both the judgemental and developmental views of
inspection. The mutual assessment of professionalism by both
teachers and inspectors will become apparent; inspection
seems to serve not only to assess professionalism but also to
define it.

Our exploration of the outcomes of inspection in the previous chapter
has not suggested that inspections can be relied upon to make a lasting
impact on a school. Whilst the inspectors have set store by the 'improvement' their work might have generated, the judgemental account seems
to have been more significant to many teachers and headteachers. Nevertheless, it appears that there will have been some more permanent effects,
some of a direct, instrumental kind, others of a more percolative, conceptual
kind.

Such tentative conclusions about the outcomes of inspection have been
based on the explicit comments of those who have been interviewed in the
case studies. However, there seems to have been a subtext which has not
always been voiced explicitly, although there have been sufficient references
to make it a legitimate issue to raise. This subtext has been about 'professionalism'. It seems to have lurked, like an iceberg, beneath the surface of the
whole project, only revealing a fraction of its substance in people's responses.

Professionalism and control

We need to try to capture this concept of professionalism. Goodlad (1984) illustrates it by alluding to 'tissues for professional use', a usage which seems to suggest the world of work, or perhaps 'quality', or an association with doctors and lawyers; 'shoes professionally mended', which perhaps suggests competence; and the television series 'The Professionals' which depicts a ruthless and tough group of people, dedicated to the public good. But beyond these common usages of the word 'professional', he argues that control of knowledge is at the heart of the concept of professionalism. He asserts that 'most occupations commonly recognised as professions control access to information valuable to the public' (p. 5).

Friedson (1973: 22) draws attention to the same point:

Professionalism might be defined as a process by which an organised occupation, usually but not always by making a claim to special esoteric competence and to concern for the quality of its work and its benefits to society, obtains the exclusive right to perform a particular kind of work, controls training for access to it, and controls the right of determining and evaluating the way the work is performed.

There are several common elements between Friedson's and Goodlad's elucidations of professionalism. Eraut (1992) identifies all of these and more in a network of related concepts, which include 'self-regulation' and 'autonomy' as well as 'service' and 'accountability'. There is a tension in their discussions between an outward-looking awareness of 'client needs' (Eraut) and a more inward-looking 'exclusive' internal control which seems to link with a notion of autonomy. Client needs suggest a market or contractual accountability, whilst internal control and autonomy seem to correspond more to professional accountability.

These two kinds of accountability have both appeared within the judgemental perception of inspection. In the worst-case scenario, the teacher or headteacher has been concerned with security of tenure, keeping a job. This is external, contractual accountability. The control lies in the employer declaring an employee as unfit for work, or in the collective employer, society (as represented by the readers of a published inspection report), making life intolerable for the employee and thus forcing a resignation. For two teachers, the inspection did bring about competence procedures. Otherwise, the worst-case scenario has been talked about as part of the mythology of inspection rather than as a reality.

A more substantial number of teachers have been preoccupied with the judgemental account from a professional point of view. This has been clearly manifested in the idea of 'justification': 'It makes you justify and think about what you're doing – that's good.'

In this justificatory position, teachers have been dependent on the inspectors, seeing them as experts. In dependency there is control. From this position, teachers attempted to 'second guess' what the inspectors wanted.

This was also the position from which teachers tried to implement the inspectors' suggestions and recommendations very quickly.

From here, teachers have often used the inspection as an opportunity to confirm, almost to define, their professional performance. One teacher went to a teacher adviser to plan and prepare her lessons for the inspectors. She was so lacking in confidence that she sought out an external model for her professional performance. We have already considered a teacher who had thought more carefully than usual about what he'd be doing during the inspection. He emphasised that he had used 'my criteria not theirs'. He appeared to have been using the inspection to focus his own idea of professional performance. We have also seen how another teacher put on a performance for the inspectors which found such approval that he sustained it afterwards. In a sense, he discovered his professionalism during the inspection.

The second teacher, who chose to define his practice according to his own criteria, discarding the inspectors' criteria, spoke in the research interview with more than a hint of bravado. His professional confidence may not have been all that secure. What seems to have allowed him to stand apart from the inspectors was his conviction that he had already passed the test of external accountability. He perceived that the parents strongly approved of his practice. He was the only teacher who, at least outwardly, rejected any idea of professional accountability to the inspection itself. Otherwise everyone revealed some sense that inspection involved a judgemental, validating account of their individual professional performance.

We have seen this individual, personal identification with the accountability of inspection repeatedly. When teachers have wanted to 'put my best foot forward' or 'be seen at my best', they have been seeing the inspection in clear judgemental terms – 'you're proving yourself'; 'my professionalism will affect what they think of the school as a whole'.

These teachers were a long way from being anonymous players in an institutional appraisal. Eraut's inclusion of 'autonomy' in the network of concepts which relate to professionalism seems open to different interpretations. We have had 'autonomous' professionals who have separated themselves from the collective accountability of the school but who have nevertheless been far from autonomous in relation to the professional expertise of the inspectors. We have had an 'autonomous' professional who has placed himself apart from the inspectors' judgements – 'my criteria not theirs' – and others who have looked for ways to displace such judgements when they have been less than palatable. And we have had 'autonomous' professionals who have been able to engage with the inspectors in 'professional discussion' where they have been willing to weigh up the significance of the inspectors' judgements without fear or favour.

Professionalism and development

In contrast with the other examples which still reveal the teachers' vulnerability to judgements and the need for validation, the last of these interpretations of autonomy equates to a developmental perception of inspection. One teacher commented that 'Any inspection demands that you sharpen up your philosophy and the rationales which underlie your teaching.'

In the research interview, this teacher seemed to be saying something subtly different from some of those who had talked of giving of their best. She seemed already to have had matured ideas of her professional performance, in terms both of why and how, and was welcoming the opportunity to sharpen and develop her thinking. This openness to the professional challenge of inspection was not all that common. Few people talked, as one headteacher did, of inspectors as 'critical friends' or of anything equivalent. But there were headteachers and teachers in most case studies who had found themselves reflecting on the inspectors' findings, not out of a struggle to understand what was expected of them, but as a stimulus to their professional development: 'I think a lot about my work anyway. One of the inspectors did talk with me about the things I think about.'

There was an important difference between the thinking of the teacher who had used his own criteria, not the inspectors', and these teachers who engaged reflectively in what the inspectors said. For the one, his professionalism was apparently untouched by the inspection. For these others, their professionalism appears to have been enriched by their willingness to participate in a developmental process.

This willingness seems usually to have been based partly on confidence, but more particularly on a capacity for reflection which already existed. The notion of 'confidence' is problematic. There were teachers in several inspections who were very nervous about the inspection, not because they feared they would somehow fail in an absolute sense, but because they feared that they would fall short of their own professional expectations, which aspired to perfection. Headteachers commented in three different cases that the teachers who had worried most had the least reason to do so. In each of these cases, the teachers concerned had engaged with the inspectors during the inspection and with the findings. These teachers may not have felt comfortable in the face of inspection, but it would be inappropriate to say that they lacked professional confidence.

It would seem to be more in order to suggest that a developmental response to inspection required a pre-existing level of professional understanding – competence rather than confidence. A key aspect of this competence seems to be that the teacher understands the significance of judgement, not as mere validation but as a basis for development. Even so, such people have needed the boost to their confidence provided by the judgemental findings of the inspection. Before engaging reflectively and developmentally, they have needed both judgemental validation and judgemental understanding.

The emergent professional

It was suggested earlier that to see the distinction between judgement and development as an oppositional dichotomy was inappropriate. There appears instead to be a progression from judgement to development. The teachers and headteachers who have talked about inspections in this research seem to have responded to them according to their position on a judgement–development progression. All have, in some way, responded first to the judgemental validation, particularly in relation to its fairness. For some, that has been the only focus of their response; for others, there have been varying degrees of engagement in the issues raised by the inspectors, either concerning their own professional performance, or, usually for more senior teachers, concerning the implications for the school as a whole. What has never been suggested is that a teacher has become more reflective as a result of an inspection. The inspection has elicited a reflective, developmental, response from a small minority who were already capable of such a response – perhaps because they understood the developmental potential of judgement. The majority was left either with lingering doubts about some aspect of what was done or said, or with a sense that 'it came and went, now no one thinks about it'.

The team who drew up the Inner London Education Authority's *Primary Language Record* (1988) depicted the learning process as a progression from dependence to independence. They saw starting readers as dependent on competent readers to unlock the meanings in the text, but over time gathering the skills to read competently for themselves. The emerging professional seems to go through a similar process. We have seen teachers and headteachers who have been dependent on external agencies in their response to inspection. They have been worried about parents' reactions and about their livelihoods. We have seen more confident, and perhaps more competent, teachers and headteachers who have transferred their dependency to the inspectors, but who have still left themselves very much at the mercy of the inspectors' processes and judgements. We have seen other teachers and headteachers who have reached a point where they feel able to challenge the inspectors. Some of these seem to have done so still from a position of dependence, rather as an adolescent wants to escape the authority of the grown-up. Others have done so because they are making professional judgements of their own which do not match those of the inspectors. And we have seen a few teachers and headteachers who have felt able to interact with inspectors more or less as equals, even though, in several cases, they have been extremely anxious.

The mature professional

If this view of the emerging 'mature' professional holds true, it brings with it several problems. Firstly, the more mature professionals do not seem to have dispensed with some of the dependencies which may have existed earlier in their professional development. Piaget (1950), in describing how young learners pass from concrete thinking towards more abstract thinking, led many of his readers to believe that learners outgrow the concrete and leave it behind. This has been strongly contested (e.g. Bruner 1967). What seems to be the case is that learners extend their range of learning approaches:

abstract thinkers still use 'concrete operations' when addressing certain new concepts. In the context of inspection, it does not seem to have been the case that those teachers who are capable of reflection and who are able to talk with inspectors as professional equals have lost their anxieties about what others might think of them. They have needed 'the concrete' of judgemental validation even if they also have the capacity to use the catalyst of inspection to move their 'abstract' professional thinking forward.

Secondly, the notion of the 'mature' professional is qualitative and thus open to argument. The teacher who chose to use his own criteria to put his 'best' performance forward during the inspection seems to have seen himself as a mature professional. The inspectors' perception of 'best' performance did not match his. Similarly, when teachers have looked to pick holes in the way that the inspectors have arrived at their judgements, this has sometimes been the result of a difference in interpretation of professional codes and criteria. More generally, such criticism has not been a 'mature' response: they have wanted to displace the inspectors' findings defensively and to avoid judgements which have been unpalatable whilst recognising, at least to an extent, that they might have been fair.

In situations where there might have been a genuine difference of professional opinion, it would have taken a third professional opinion to adjudicate. Theoretically, this was the point of having a team of inspectors. The corporate view should have ironed out any idiosyncrasies of professional interpretation amongst the inspectors, thus providing a consistent point of view in the face of any alternative viewpoints expressed by teachers or headteachers. In actuality, the corporate view did not always pertain, either because the team leader's view dominated or because individual inspectors reported separately within the team framework. The idea of the 'corporate view' only reinforces the point that professional opinion is essentially negotiable. There would be no need for a corporate view if the judgements being made were fixed. This has caused some difficulty in the inspections carried out strictly to the Ofsted framework. The framework, and the insistence on using inspectors who have no previous knowledge of the school, seem to have created a sense that the inspection is somehow fact, as opposed to opinion. We have looked at this problem of 'pseudo-scientism' before. The reality has been that each inspection has had to achieve a consensus of opinion which accepts it as 'fair', whereby the teachers and headteachers, as a collegiate group, have recognised the findings of the inspectors as legitimate, reliable and valid.

This 'negotiated' professional view was particularly prominent in the case study where the inspectors departed from a purely judgemental agenda early on the first day. From then on, they adopted a developmental agenda, offering suggestions which the teachers were free to dispense with if they were found not to work. The report for this inspection was to be written by teachers and inspectors together, as a collaborative venture. But negotiation has taken place to some extent in almost every case, as the inspectors have tailored their findings to match their perception of what the school was ready to hear.

In addition to the qualitative, and hence subjective, interpretation of what was and what was not 'mature' professional performance, there was an added complication when the level of the inspector's professional maturity did not match that of the teacher. We have seen how many of the inspections had a particular victim – the scapegoat. The teachers in this position were usually unable to understand why they had been picked out for opprobrium, or did not even recognise that they had been. The most extreme example of this was when a teacher was 'put down' in the staff feedback meeting with the comment, 'that's tough'. The inspector and the teacher in this case were on different planets and could not communicate.

My argument has been that professional maturation is not a question of replacing the need for validating judgement with a confident capacity for development but rather a question of adding a reflective, developmental, capability to a continuing need for validating judgements. This seems to require a particular understanding of how judgement and development are related. It appears to have held true not only for teachers but also for inspectors. What appears to have happened in this latter case is that the inspector had lost a sensitivity to the validating dimension of the situation. She said that she 'found it quite amusing'. Her own professional autonomy seems to have reached a point where she did not feel accountable to those she was inspecting.

The professionalism of inspectors

Although this inspector's autonomy may have gone too far, there has been a sense that the inspector's professional maturity does reach a point of complete independence: 'My accountability is to myself – I like to do the job properly.' This comment was echoed by another inspector, but with an important addition: 'My accountability is for myself – I've got to live with myself and then with others, especially the school.'

Several writers about inspectors and advisers have pointed out that inspection has an inward-looking quality, whereby judgements are trapped in a kind of black hole. Pearce (1986) suggests that a professional can only be held accountable by a professional which suggests that one of these two professionals can only ultimately be accountable to herself. Wilcox (1992) raises a similar point and also considers the idea of 'connoisseurship' in inspection, implying that judgements are a matter of taste adjudicated by seasoned professionals. Winkley (1985) asks whether the inspector achieves the goals which are set for him, or those he sets for himself. He also makes much of the fact that outside of the full inspection setting, many inspectors work alone as advisers and that they do not readily come together in teams. This separateness was particularly evident in the case where five inspectors wrote separate reports. Bolam, Smith and Canter (1978: 81) pick up on the self-serving nature of inspection work: 'General inspections are of value to advisers because they allow a deeper understanding of the school than is otherwise possible.' Delves and Watts (1982: 133) identify an assumption – that 'the inspectorate knows best and the teachers will be judged on the extent to which they have "got it right"'.

Although there has been a recognition amongst the inspectors that they are the ultimate adjudicators – 'our judgements cannot be challenged' – there has been an equally prevalent concern to 'get it right' themselves. The comment quoted above, 'I like to do the job properly' has been made repeatedly:

'There's a lot of pressure on us to do the job properly while we're there – a responsibility to get it right.'

'People need to know what they have to do and be competent (not expert) to do the job.'

'They have to get it right for themselves and for the team.'

'My dominant concern was to get it right as team leader.'

The inspectors who made these comments were revealing some of the same insecurities that teachers expressed about their performance. They were suggesting that they were also being judged. Comments made by headteachers and teachers confirm that this was so: 'A good inspector needs to be someone with an interest in the success of the inspection process'; or 'When they'd gone, the opinion was that we'd been done by a professional team.'

These comments echo those made in the context of our discussion of credibility earlier. The inspectors may have had autonomy in making their professional judgements, but they still felt accountable. Most inspectors have mentioned their sense of accountability to the teachers in the school. Many have also mentioned the children, particularly the notion of their getting a 'fair deal'. Some have referred to an accountability to colleagues, particularly those in the team, and a few have mentioned their own managers. One inspector was nevertheless adamant that he did not feel accountable to Ofsted or to the government.

All of my case studies took place before the statutory Ofsted inspections began in primary schools. The situation now is that Ofsted's accredited inspectors are held accountable to Ofsted. They are monitored by another tier of professionals who are accountable to the Chief Inspector who is appointed by, and is accountable to, the Secretary of State. There were signs in the case studies which used the Ofsted framework that inspectors were losing some autonomy, at least in terms of procedures and criteria. Nevertheless, the judgements of these inspectors were still unchallenged and it is difficult to see how this will change in any fundamental way under the new Ofsted arrangements. Inspectors will be anxious about losing their accreditation if they fail to follow correct procedures and cannot point to the evidence on which their judgements are based. But their judgements will still be unique and unchallengeable. It will take someone else's professional judgement to say whether these judgements are secure. As Juvenal (*c.* AD 100) said, '*Quis custodiet ipsos custodes?*' ('Who looks after those who do the looking after?') The circularity remains. The garden may be less secret, but its keys will still be difficult to obtain.

The inspectors in this project seem to have conformed to the pattern that existed amongst teachers. Although they may have reached a level of professional maturity where they have considerable autonomy, their need for the validation of judgement has nevertheless applied. Their desire to do 'a good job' has been, at least to an extent, to sustain their credibility in the face of teachers and colleagues. But at the same time, we have seen that, as mature professionals, their view of inspection has tended to be a developmental one.

Indeed, some inspectors seem to have wanted to resist any perception of themselves as being involved in a validation exercise. This has been particularly evident in their resistance to the dependency implied in being seen as experts: 'There is a great danger in our being looked to for an expert body of knowledge.' Winkley (1985: 224) picks this up when he says that: 'Autonomy ought to mean freedom to learn – open country rather than castle walls.' Instead, they seem to have been trying to treat teachers as equal partners: 'I wouldn't want to go through the week without a professional dialogue.'

This seems to have caused tension in several of the inspections. Many inspectors seem to have been making their judgements as a means to a developmental end. Meanwhile, many of the teachers have not been ready to see past the judgements. A mismatch has emerged: the position of some teachers on the pathway between judgement and development has not coincided with the position of some inspectors. Some inspectors have been more sensitive to this mismatch than others.

We need to be careful about an assumption that inspectors have been entitled to autonomy on the basis of their professional maturity. We have seen how such autonomy might be abused. The position of inspectors within the overall professional hierarchy suggests that they should be mature. The inspectors themselves have not always felt confident of their credentials to fulfil the role, nor have they always revealed their competence. There have been two contradictory ways in which the inspectors have dealt with this. In some situations, we have seen how they have avoided dialogue and have hidden behind their status or behind the ritual of the inspection process. This suggests a regression into a judgemental mode and seems to fit the progression we have seen amongst teachers: the levels of confidence and competence determine the capacity to take a developmental stance. Conversely, in a few situations, there has been an avoidance of judgements. The reluctance to accept the expert position is open to such an interpretation. It would be safer to engage in dialogue without judgement than with it.

Whose professionalism?

Writers such as Winkley (1985), Schön (1987), Gray (1988), Heller (1988), Harland (1990), Easen (1991), Mezirow (1992), and Wilcox (1992), who have explored the potential developmental effects of either evaluative or advisory activity, have stressed the importance of negotiation and a sense of ownership. Easen (1991) advocates a style of working in which partners can construct shared understandings and meanings. Herein lies one of the key issues. We have been faced with participants in inspections who have only rarely been close to operating in partnership. Nevertheless, the process of each inspection has been instrumental in constructing understandings and meanings. What seems to have been critical has been the extent to which such understandings and meanings have, or have not, been shared.

The fluctuating perceptions of inspection as sometimes judgemental, sometimes developmental, sometimes both, and the consequent constructions of meaning may have been dependent on the professional maturity of those taking part and the match between participants' levels of professional maturity. This is to use the notion of professionalism to illustrate the processes and outcomes of the case studies. However, we have also seen that an understanding of professionalism is itself constructed by inspection. The 'professional job' which the inspectors were trying to do was not one which was well defined prior to each of the case studies. The teachers only knew what to expect from what they had been told by the inspectors. So the professional performance of the inspectors was defined anew by each inspection and, as we have seen in previous chapters, teachers were quick to criticise when they felt that the credibility, consistency or sensitivity of the inspection broke down. Simultaneously, teachers were discovering expectations of their own professional performance which they had not previously known or understood.

To an extent, the Ofsted framework (1992, revised 1994) has curtailed the scope for the negotiation of professionalism in inspection. There is a code of conduct which outlines a set of principles:

- honesty, clarity, consistency and objectivity in the framing and communicating of judgements;
- concern for accuracy and respect for evidence;
- confidentiality in handling all information acquired during an inspection;
- courtesy, fairness and openness in discussion when dealing with all individuals and groups encountered in the course of an inspection;
- sensitivity to the circumstances of the school and of all individuals or groups connected with it;
- respect for the integrity of teachers, pupils, parents and governors;
- recognition that the interests and welfare of pupils are the first priority in relation to anything inspectors observe or about which they are informed;
- sensitivity to the impact of judgements on others.

There is also a list of criteria by which inspectors' judgements can be evaluated: security, first-handedness, reliability, validity, comprehensiveness, and corporateness. Every aspect to be inspected is also governed by explicit criteria. However, the effect of this is to raise the negotiation of meaning to another level. These criteria all have to be interpreted; none of them is susceptible to positivist measurement. The fact that Ofsted inspections are themselves monitored (inspected) still does not remove the circularity. The whole process is dependent on the credibility of professional judgement, and the credibility of professional judgement is defined by the process.

Is there any way to break out of this circularity? Inspection has long been dogged by the notion of 'good practice' – a construct of what teachers ought to do which inspectors have carried in their heads and only revealed to teachers as they have applied it. The focus of the Ofsted framework on learning outcomes has helped to break this down, although the re-emergence of the quality of teaching – as opposed to the quality of learning – in revisions to the framework shows how difficult it is to sustain. The professionalism of inspection is the professionalism of peers. Although there have been frequent references to the children by both teachers and inspectors, there is still some way to go before the idea of service to the client is consistently and rigorously applied. There is a danger that the ritualisation and mythology of inspection, strengthened as they have been by the advent of Ofsted, will generate new orthodoxies which will stand in the way of the quest for serving the best interests of young learners and for new ways of judging whether those interests are being served.

10 INSPECTION
ILLUMINATED

In this chapter, the themes and issues which have been identified are brought together to form a picture of inspection.

When an inspection takes place, a group of people, each of whom carries the title 'inspector', visits a school for a limited number of days. Before their visit, the inspectors will probably have familiarised themselves with any written information the school has provided. During the visit, the inspectors gather information and make judgements about the strengths and weaknesses of the school. At the end of their visit, they inform the school about what they have found.

Myth and meaning

Although, no doubt, there are commonsense understandings of what inspection is about, the whole process of each of the case studies has been dominated by each participant's attempt to make sense of what has been going on and what has been expected. Neither the inspectors nor those within the school – headteachers, teachers and governors – seem to have had a particularly clear formulation of where inspection might fit into a wider picture of accountability. Whilst people have been able to allude to external audiences, such as parents, the local education authority or even the government, for any report which the inspection might generate, they have more consistently made sense of the inspection in terms of their own particular circumstances.

People make sense of things in relation to what they already know. As far as the headteachers and teachers in the case studies were concerned, few of them had experienced an inspection before. As a result they were dependent on hearsay for any preconception of what inspection might entail. This hearsay appears to have been predominantly negative in tone, depicting inspection as a kind of monster. Its strength was such that it opened up their deeper insecurities and generated high levels of anxiety. As such it took on the archetypal dimensions of myth and mythology. The fact that each inspection followed a remarkably consistent pattern added to this mythology, as inspectors were seen to be playing out a ritualised choreography whose purposes were not always clear even to the inspectors themselves.

Judgement and development

For those within the school, the experience of the inspection itself was generally more significant than any wider purpose or rationale. Nevertheless, everyone recognised, at some level, that judgement lay at the heart of the inspection. The experience has been likened to taking an examination and to participating in a courtroom trial.

Inspectors have persistently emphasised development; it must be conceded, I also used to have a particularly developmental perception of what inspection was about. Although judgement can be used diagnostically to underpin recommendations or suggestions for improvement, there can be no escaping the centrality of judgement itself in the perceptions of teachers and headteachers. For them, the business of inspection has been first and foremost to pass – to receive a not-guilty verdict. Despite a notable absence of concern about whom these inspectors have represented, there has been nothing trivial about this; the fear of failure has been very powerful.

Professionalism

In their attempts to manage their own morale and that of the teachers, headteachers have emphasised the potential for development in the inspection process. Some teachers have been able to focus on this aspect of the process, particularly those who already had sufficient maturity as professionals to be able to reflect on what the inspectors were saying.

The notion of professionalism seems to have been central to the meaning of inspection. The inspectors have been making an assessment of the professional performance of the teachers, the headteacher and of the school as a whole. The teachers have attempted to perform in relation to their understanding of professionalism and of their assumptions of the professionalism that the inspectors might have been looking for. At the same time, the inspectors have been trying to carry out the inspection in relation to their own ideas of a professional job; the teachers have stood ready to criticise if the inspectors fall short. Unfortunately, because most of the teachers have not experienced inspection before and because the inspectors have not previously worked together as a team, there could be no predetermined consensus about what this professional performance was. The inspection became a professional negotiation, mediated by principles such as fairness and by interpretations and expectations which were particular to the time and place.

There does seem to have been a circularity about inspection and the professionalism which has given it meaning. However, the participants were not completely trapped in a secret garden. The headteachers and teachers were working from an accumulation of experience of managing children's learning and the inspectors were bringing their perceptions and expectations from work in other places. The processes have been governed by criteria, sometimes explicit, sometimes implicit. Whether or not they have followed the trial, outsiders would have been able to understand the difference between 'guilty' and 'not guilty'. Whether that verdict is sufficiently related to the real interests of the true clients of the school – the children – will depend on continuing progress in the notoriously difficult task of assessing and judging educational outcomes.

Victims and scapegoats

Inspection seems to reveal a hierarchy of professionals. This hierarchy has been determined by a combination of confidence and competence. This has proved to be a difficult combination to untangle. An aspect of confidence seems to have lain in an awareness of what greater competence might entail. As a result, some of the less confident participants in inspection have been those who have had the greatest insight into the complexity of a genuinely 'good' professional performance, whether as headteachers, teachers or inspectors. There have been other participants who have been more confident but on the basis of more limited aspirations. The picture has been confused by the fact that people's confidence can be more apparent than real.

It has been possible to identify a small minority of teachers and headteachers who have been ready to engage in the inspection process knowing that their performance was safely outside of any danger zone. These participants have been able to welcome the developmental potential of the inspection. They have still needed the validation of the inspection's verdict and a pre-existing understanding of the significance of judgement. There have also been inspectors who have known that they have conducted the inspection well and have been able to reflect both on how they might improve on their performance next time and on the insights the inspection has given them into professionalism itself.

Most participants have not been as confident about their performance, probably because they have not been as competent. For them the verdict of the inspection has been their main preoccupation. They have presented themselves somewhat passively, dependent on the inspectors. They have breathed sighs of relief that they have passed the examination. For the inspectors among them, they have looked to ensure that their performance would escape serious criticism from the teachers and that their credibility would remain intact.

But there have been casualties. One or two of these have not been incompetent. The strain of performing to their maximum level has undermined their health. However, for each inspection, there has been at least one teacher who has been cast in the role of scapegoat. The inspectors seem to have needed to identify a worst performer and have always made sure that the headteacher knows this person's identity. In some cases, the teacher has not been informed, although someone else in the school consistently has been. In others, the consequences for the teacher have been devastating, in some instances leading to long-term absence.

Institutional or individual?

The custom and practice of inspection portrays it as an institutional appraisal. There has been a convention that written reports following inspections would not name individual teachers. The fact that individual teachers have identified themselves as having 'failed' in the case studies of this project suggests that this institutional emphasis has also failed. This has fed the negative mythology of inspection, which is likely to contribute to individual anxiety in subsequent inspections elsewhere.

Teachers and headteachers have consistently felt anxious about their own performance as they have prepared for and participated in their inspections. They have then looked for references to themselves in the report. The inspection process itself has been made up of an accumulation of one-to-one exchanges. There has been a convention that inspectors will generally observe singly and interviews have generally been held one-to-one. It is not surprising that individual teachers have had difficulty with the institutional nature of inspection. They have known that their performance has contributed to the whole and have been keen not to let the side down, but they have also wanted to know how they have done as individuals. The issue of individual feedback has featured significantly in their comments.

Despite this strong personalisation of inspection in the minds and feelings of individual teachers, the effect of inspection has generally been to consolidate staff solidarity. In one case, it even had the effect of uniting a previously fragmented staff. The staffs have not generally turned on the victims of the inspections, nor do they appear to have resented the success of particular colleagues. The increased cohesion of the school staff seems to have been caused by a sense of having come through a stressful experience together.

Corporate or individual?

Just as the inspection is of the whole school, so are the findings intended to be the corporate judgements of the whole team. Despite considerable emphasis by inspectors on working together to agree their findings, the case studies have placed some doubt on the security of this corporate view. It is difficult to see how a number of separate judgements could have been made into one. In the negotiation of a consensus strongly held opinions have been discarded. The casting vote of the lead inspector has been used quite frequently, particularly since the report has been written after the team has disbanded. There have been several examples of individual inspectors feeding back individual views and of individual judgements feeding into reports without significant team deliberations.

That the judgements of inspection are necessarily individual interpretations of evidence, often more intuitively than methodically weighed, has only served to demonstrate the essentially qualitative nature of the process. The involvement of a number of inspectors seems to have served to make the findings of the inspections more secure overall, but it has not stopped individual teachers ascribing certain judgements to individual inspectors. It is not surprising that teachers have often seen the inspectors as separate individuals, although they have been less likely to do so when the team has been effectively led.

Technical and emotional

The inspectors' business has been to gather sufficient evidence to make reliable judgements about the school's performance. The pattern of this evidence-gathering has been remarkably consistent. It has involved reading documents, scrutinising children's work, interviewing teachers, and observing in classrooms and around the school. The inspectors' performance in this evidence-gathering process has been a mixture of science and craft. There has been little consensus about the value or method of some of their evidence-gathering, particularly the analysis of documentation and samples of children's work. The teachers have attempted, with varying degrees of success, to predict what the inspectors would be looking for and to perform accordingly.

However, to put forward a valid account of the process of inspection in terms of a cold, dispassionate description of technical activity is like describing a living being merely anatomically. Inspection has engendered strong feelings. These feelings have affected the nature of the evidence the inspectors have gathered, the way they have interpreted it, the way they have communicated their findings, and the likelihood that these findings would be accepted, either as a judgemental verdict or as a contribution to development.

There have been identifiable dynamics of feeling in relation to the stages of the process. From the school's point of view, there has been a gathering anxiety as the inspection visit has approached, with maximum stress at the very outset of the visit. During the visit, there have been highs and lows as teachers have had particular exchanges with inspectors and in relation to their own perceptions of their performance. As the visit has progressed, there has been a growing tiredness, which has often affected the children as well. At the end of the visit, the headteacher's experience of the oral feedback appears often to have been a sustained emotional climax of Wagnerian proportions. The departure of the inspectors has signalled a massive release, described by some as a 'catharsis', leaving people flat and exhausted. For many, this flatness has been prolonged over a number of weeks, described as 'post-inspection syndrome'.

These emotional dynamics have not been universally shared. There has been a minority of teachers who have not taken the inspection so seriously and have not been so affected. However, in general, the intensity of feeling has indicated how personally vulnerable people have felt in the face of inspection. The experience could be likened to running a marathon, or being in the dock during a long trial, or sustaining a non-stop stage performance.

For the inspectors, the emotional dynamics of the inspection have gener-ally been in relation to their emerging judgements of the school's perform-ance, although they have sometimes been complicated by tensions within the team, caused usually by insecurities in the position of the team's leader. In addition to the identification of particular weak teachers who have some-times become a dustbin for the inspectors' negativity, there have been highs and lows as the inspectors have searched collectively for their perception of the right verdict for the school as a whole. Judgements of practice have often been accompanied by surprisingly strong feelings. There has been anger at particular poor practice and elation at particular strong practice. At the same time, there has often been a kind of collective depression when inspectors have started to recognise patterns of weaker performance. In several in-stances, an inspector, usually the leader of the team, has had to bring col-leagues back to a less emotional position by emphasising the need to look for a balance of evidence.

The feelings engendered by inspection seem to have come in part from the horror stories that are told about it. However, they have also come from its challenge to people's self-esteem. People do volunteer to subject themselves to examinations and to perform in amateur dramatics but usually do so with some confidence that they will emerge with added credit. These inspections have left little choice; there has been a randomness about where they hap-pened which seems to have added to a sense of powerlessness in those who were to be inspected. This has probably made it more difficult for teachers to see their positive potential, despite the headteachers' encouragement to do so in most of the case studies. That the judgemental view of inspection has tended to defeat a more developmental view in the perception of most teachers prob-ably does not reflect a true balance between a pessimistic and optimistic world view. It takes a certain excess of enthusiasm to welcome an assessment of one's professional performance when one has had no control over its timing and when one may feel that there is plenty else to be worrying about.

Displacement

Whilst most inspectors have wanted to emphasise development as a worth-while end to the less palatable means of inspection, many teachers and headteachers have focused on the judgements of inspection and have looked to find ways to undermine them. The extreme form of this has been subversion, such as through a headteacher's failure to share the inspectors' procedures with his staff, or a teacher's failure to bring her planning sheets to school, or a teacher repeatedly avoiding the inspectors by deploying a student in her place. More generally, it has been through headteachers and teachers questioning the reliability of the evidence base; or by criticising inconsistencies in the way different inspectors in the same team have worked; and, particularly, by questioning the credentials and credibility of particular inspectors, especially with reference to their behaviour in the classroom. This last issue combines the technical performance of inspectors with their interpersonal style. What has counted in the classroom has been the way in which the inspectors have demonstrated an ability to relate to the children. Teachers have sometimes claimed that an inspector's failure to behave appropriately in the classroom has affected their own performance.

The inspectors' interpersonal style has also been particularly important in the context of interviews. Teachers have complained that inspectors have not been interested in what they had to say, or that the interview has been more of an interrogation than a discussion. Whilst this might have been attributable as much to the teacher's anxiety as to the inspector's animosity, it still illustrates how the technical objective of evidence-gathering has been subject to the way in which the emotional agenda has been managed. An interview which has been poorly managed on a human level has given the teachers the opportunity to criticise, and at times to reject, the validity of the information-sharing which was meant to have taken place.

Relationships

With people's performances being so subject to their feelings, the management of the emotional agenda of the inspection has taken on particular importance. Despite allusions in some of the earlier case studies to closing the gap between inspectors and teachers, and despite some suggestions in the wider educational context at the time the research began that inspectors and schools should work in partnership, the fundamental relationship between inspectors and schools has been a subject–object relationship. If the inspectors have been required to arrive at firm judgements about the practice of those within the school, it has not been possible for their relationship to be other than hierarchical. It is therefore not surprising that there have been relatively few headteachers or teachers who have been able to treat these fellow professionals on an equal footing.

The lead inspector's and the headteacher's roles in establishing the best possible working relationships for the inspection have been central. Despite some attempts by headteachers to take control overall, there has only been one occasion where the inspectors have been close to losing control. In one other case the inspector–school relationship was particularly weak. In this instance, the headteacher may have played a part in keeping the inspection going. Even in this worst case, the verdict of the inspectors was still seen by most of the staff as legitimate.

Any particular secret of managing relationships effectively during inspections has been difficult to unearth. The Ofsted code of conduct talks of 'courtesy, fairness and openness in discussion'; of 'sensitivity to the circumstances of the school'; 'respect for the integrity of teachers'; and 'sensitivity to the impact of judgements on others'. These elements have not always been separately identifiable in the case studies but, where good relationships appear to have pertained, they have existed collectively. The key difference seems to have occurred when there has been an open acknowledgement that a human, emotional, agenda has existed. In the cases where relationships appear to have been consistently more secure, this acknowledgement was deliberate and occurred at the outset of the inspection process, in the briefing sessions. In some other cases, an acknowledgement occurred by accident, through chance informal moments. When this happened, teachers spoke as if their perception of the inspection and the inspectors had been transformed: 'My God, he's human!'

Ritual

The management of feelings and the search for meaning in the inspections have come together in the form of ritual. In two cases, teachers have admitted to being disconcerted by the formality of inspectors whom they had previously worked with in a more informal advisory context. The difficulty of conveying judgements in the face of feeling has generated ritualised behaviour amongst the inspectors, particularly at the most difficult moments: the initial entry to the school and the oral feedback to the headteacher, which could be seen as the climax of the inspection process. When there have been difficult moments during the inspection, the inspectors have similarly pulled away from more intimate relationships into a more formal role. To help them in this, they have also generally dressed formally.

Ritual may have been an important way of masking feeling. It has also been a way of giving predictable shape to the whole process. The way in which the inspection will be carried out has often been 'rehearsed' by the lead inspector in a briefing to the staff. Where this has happened, the teachers have felt more comfortable. They may not always have understood why something was going to happen but they have at least had the security of knowing what was going to happen. In similar vein, a church congregation may not know why bells are rung at particular moments during a high church Eucharist, but the predictability of the pattern of the service gives it its own meaning and offers a certain security. Where inspectors have behaved inconsistently in relation to other inspectors, teachers have been confused and have questioned the reliability of the inspection.

There has been a curious tension here. Whilst a consistent, ritualised, pattern of inspection has given the experience a coherence and meaning in terms of the event it was described to be, it has been when teachers and inspectors have made contact across the ritual boundaries and when inspectors have shown that they can make human contact with children in the classroom that the inspection has somehow come alive. Some kind of a sensitive balance appears to have been necessary, a balance between the formal and the informal.

Inescapably it has been the inspectors' responsibility to manage this balance. The teachers have remained in the passive position, the objects of the inspection. The inspectors have had to reveal themselves as 'also human' without undermining the credibility of their position. When one inspector admitted that he was very shy, he seems to have overstepped this boundary; the teacher appreciated his honesty but nevertheless felt that it was his responsibility to manage this problem if he was to command respect as an inspector.

Tailoring

The inspection teams' search for a balance in relationships combined with their search for a balance in the evidence seems sometimes to have led them to work harder to find strengths in a school when their overall perception has become negative. In several cases, individual inspectors have still been wondering well after the event whether their reported picture of the school was too kind or not kind enough. This seems to suggest that their overall assessment of a school may have been mediated by feeling. This suggestion has been strengthened by the significant number of instances where the inspectors did not report everything they might have done, because it would not have helped the school. This matching of what was reported to a notion of what the school might have been able to bear underlines the qualitative nature of the whole process and shows that, despite a growing focus on assessing the school's performance, the inspectors were simultaneously assessing the school's developmental performance and potential.

Ownership

The inspectors' tailoring of their findings to match what they thought the school might have been ready to hear fits a wider intention to establish ownership of their findings. Although one case seems to have indicated that most members of a school's staff can accept the inspectors' verdict even in the face of inconsistent procedures and poor relationships, the teachers who felt most criticised in this case did not accept these criticisms. Ultimately, the inspectors' preoccupation with doing a professional job, the consistency and effectiveness of their procedures and the achievement of appropriate relationships seem to have been focused on the successful communication of their findings and recommendations to those within the school.

Inspectors have revealed that they have generally kept either the teachers or the headteacher in their mind's eye when they have written their reports, although sometimes the governors have been seen as the principal audience. In both written and oral feedback, they have wanted to secure a full understanding of their findings. To achieve this, they have usually leaked their judgements in advance, through conversations with subject coordinators and with the headteacher. There seems consistently to have been a developmental intention behind this negotiation of meaning together with, at times, a desire to test how well their findings are likely to be received.

The school's ownership of the inspectors' findings has been established, more often than not, and sometimes to a substantial extent, by the self-evaluation undertaken by the school beforehand. In several cases, the school has claimed that it knew what the inspectors would say beforehand. There were even instances where the inspectors reported judgements which had been fed to them by the school. Inspection then became a validation of the school's perception of itself. However, headteachers and teachers have also suggested that the school would not have evaluated itself so rigorously had an inspection not been forthcoming. Moreover, in every case the school has acknowledged that there was something the inspectors had identified or clarified which had not been fully recognised beforehand. Indeed, in the two schools whose prior view of themselves appeared to have been most closely matched by the inspectors' view, the inspection seems to have stirred action to tackle issues which had been too long avoided.

Distortion

Apart from the subjectivity of the inspectors' judgements, and their mediation in the context of the corporate dynamics of the inspection team, the question of how true a picture an inspection can have provided has been further complicated by the effect of the inspection on the school's usual performance. There have been several examples of how practice in the classroom and across the school as a whole has been altered by either the prospect or the presence of the inspectors.

The significance of the issue of distortion is dependent on what is expected of inspection. If the expectation is that the inspection will identify the strengths and weaknesses of a single school, then the success of that inspection might be seen to lie in the acceptability of the inspection report as a recognisable account, with recommendations that ask for appropriate and realistic future action. In the course of the process, there have sometimes been opportunities for teachers to point out the unreliability of some of the evidence. Moreover, the inspectors' accumulation of evidence, tested against different sources, will have helped to create a reliable picture. Although teachers have pointed out anomalies between reported practice and what they would consider to be their usual practice, there has only been one case where these have come close to being sufficient to challenge the overall findings of the report. Even in this case, the staff saw the overall report as 'fair'.

If, on the other hand, the inspection is expected to provide a reliable comparison with other schools, then its report may need to satisfy more robust tests of its validity and reliability than is provided by the successful negotiation of legitimacy and recognisability within the school. From a positivist point of view, it could be argued that, since inspectors always affect the context they are inspecting, inspection reports consistently describe distorted provision and are thus reliably comparable. However, this argument does not really stand up to further scientific scrutiny. There are just too many variables. The distortion would not be constant, nor would the tailoring, since both are determined by the human responses of both the inspectors and those within the school. At the end of the day, inspection cannot satisfy scientific tests for proof or truth. The external validity of an inspection report has to be underwritten by the same test as its internal validity: its overall acceptability to those who have been inspected. If the school has seen the report as fair, who else is to say that it wasn't?

External accountability

External accountability needs to be acknowledged in any study of inspection. Yet this did not feature strongly in the interviews. When prompted, people have acknowledged the existence of government and LEAs, but their anxiety about the worst possible consequence of inspection – the loss of livelihood – has, if mentioned at all, been expressed in terms of a loss of professional credibility rather than in terms of dismissal. Teachers have generally been more preoccupied with the immediacy of the inspection than with its wider rationale.

They have occasionally acknowledged that the governors have a part to play. Although they have not been a focus of this project, where governors have been interviewed, they have seemed generally to be rather detached from the inspections in question. They have not felt themselves to be inspected, nor have they had a clear view of what the inspection might mean to them. They seem to have seen it as a matter for the professionals; they have shown an interest in the headteacher's and teachers' view of what has transpired, and expected any necessary action plan to be submitted to them by the headteacher.

However, any view of the value of inspection which might have been revealed by this research needs to be placed in this wider context. It may be that, even if the benefits to the school of its inspection are seen as limited, in a system-wide context the value of inspection would be seen more positively.

The illusion of objectivity

In the context of an emerging managerialist culture of accountability to the market, inspection is meant to be seen as an authoritative assessment of a school's performance. It may also be seen as a weapon in a war on alleged low standards, which implies that it is intended to have some developmental impact. This project has confirmed that these perceptions look to have taken root within the schools, though more subconsciously than consciously. Only once has anyone asked 'who do the inspectors think they are?' and even that comment had been prompted more by the inspectors' insensitivity than by any fundamental questioning of the whole inspection business. Teachers and headteachers seem to have accepted that they will be inspected, resigned to their number being called.

At the same time, there have been repeated reminders that the process falls short of being a hard-edged assessment of the school's performance. The technical process has been much tempered by the emotional; judgements have been conditional and negotiated; and the calibrations of scientific measurement have been conspicuous by their absence.

However, at the core of the inspection process there has been a sharp edge. Apart from one case, which might perhaps be seen to have reflected a past advisory culture, each of the inspections has made a core judgement of whether the school was, or was not, providing an acceptable education for the children in its care. The teachers and headteachers appear to have recognised this more clearly than the inspectors. Throughout the project, they have revealed high levels of anxiety about the central verdict of the inspection, such that, for a majority, the balance of the inspection has tipped towards judgement and away from development. Whilst, under Ofsted procedures, the language of the reporting of judgements has become more explicit, the inspectors have continued to emphasise a developmental intent, seeing their judgements as diagnostic – a means to a developmental end – rather than as definitive.

The decision about whether a school passes or fails is not as clear-cut as observing water and identifying the freezing point at which liquid becomes solid. Nevertheless, it seems to have carried the same clear-cut message. The irony has been that the inspectors seem to have needed to assess the school's developmental position as part of their judgement of its current standing. Whilst the validating judgement of inspection may have been stronger than its developmental contribution, this validating judgement seems to have needed a validation of its developmental dynamic.

The processes and outcomes of inspection in primary schools

At the outset of the research, I had a picture of inspection which was dominated by developmental expectations and which conveniently ignored the powerful emotions it arouses. It was essentially a mechanistic view, displacing the untidiness of the event of inspection with an idea, perhaps an ideal, of inspection as a generator of subsequent developmental thought and activity.

As the project has progressed, the complexity of inspection has become more and more apparent. There do appear to have been some of the kind of outcomes that I originally had in mind. There has usually been an action plan associated with the inspection's recommendations; teachers have attributed identifiable changes in their practice to the inspection, although some of these might have been unlikely to persist because they were not fully under-stood; and the inspections themselves appear to have prompted schools to write policy documents, to sharpen their short-term planning, and to recon-sider the role of subject coordinators. However, it quickly became apparent that a simple attribution to inspection of subsequent changes was very dif-ficult. While many people were convinced that their inspection would have some longer-term benefit, others were more dismissive, claiming that the school would reach the same place without an inspection, or that develop-ment should be attributed to some other cause, such as National Curriculum implementation or statutory assessment.

The relationship between these instrumental outcomes and the inspection itself seems to have depended on a notion of assent. Teachers and headteachers have been prepared to do things differently as a result of the inspection be-cause they have been convinced that they should. They might have been con-vinced by the status of the inspectors, as agents of the LEA or as experts, or because they had learned something from them. This is to distinguish between people having acted because they were told to – strategic compliance – and because they understood why and wanted to. This is not necessarily to deny that strategic compliance might not subsequently be consolidated into a learned compliance.

That the learning from inspection might have been limited can be attrib-uted to the anxiety which has surrounded it. Fear is an inhibitor of learning. Only those who have been able to stand outside the fear of the validating judgement of the inspection have been well placed to learn from it. These were the people who had sufficient professional maturity to be able to reflect and to engage developmentally with the inspector's findings. Otherwise, the preoccupation has been with the validating judgement itself.

But it has been the assent of teachers and headteachers to the verdict of the inspectors which has always been the key. The inspection had to be seen as fair and legitimate both in the way that it was conducted and in its findings if it was to succeed. This legitimacy has had to operate on both a technical and an emotional level. It is of interest to note that Ofsted saw a need to introduce a code of conduct for inspections when it published the second edition of the framework. By doing so, they acknowledged the human agenda and confirmed the ethical dimension of the professionalism which has been at the core of the case studies. Where the inspectors have failed to satisfy the technical or emotional requirements of the inspection process, however subjectively they have been defined, the teachers have been able to displace the validity of the inspection.

Perhaps the most fascinating aspect of the project has been to discover the extent to which inspection has proved to be both a process and an out-come. In the process of constructing a picture of the school, it is also being constructed itself, as the participants struggle, often rather painfully, to make sense of what it is and what it purports to be doing. Whilst it seems to be accepted externally as a way into the secret garden, it seems itself to remain very much within the garden and may indeed be sustaining the secrecy it seeks to reveal.

Inspection constructed

So what is inspection? Although it has been possible to find many common elements between the 12 cases in the project, inspection, as a generic term, must be seen to be a collection of inspections, each of which is separate. Otherwise we might miss the essential particularity of each inspection as it is constructed.

An inspection may, in many ways, be likened to a musical performance. A group of musicians (inspectors and teachers) come together to make music. Now that there is an Ofsted framework, the musicians will usually be playing from a score. Even so, there is plenty of room for different interpretations. In the earlier case studies of this project, the performance was more improvised – like jazz – but there were still rules and conventions.

The mood of the piece can be set by the way that it is played; players have to take their cues from other players; there will sometimes be harmony and sometimes discord, particularly if some players are less competent or confident in their musical skills; those performers who are aware of the audience will respond to their reactions. Although the performance may be characterised as an event, it is also an experience; there is an ebb and flow of insight and feeling. The performance will have an immediate impact on its participants, but it may resonate for a long time afterwards, perhaps restructuring future experience. If so, the participants may be said to have learned from it. They may not be able to predict at the time how significant it might become. There may be some who were unmoved by the experience but who find themselves humming, a long time afterwards, a few bars of the music that was played.

Any analogy can be overworked. However, many of the tensions, paradoxes and polarities of inspection can be found. There is a coming together of people with different levels of emotional confidence and technical competence; a sense that the quality is both already there but also needing to be discovered; the need for approval but a potential for improvement; an awareness of form but room for interpretation; and an interplay between the private and the public.

The pervasiveness of judgement in inspection is not reflected in the same way in a musical performance. Music does have its critics outside – the external agents of accountability – but in inspection the critics are also inside. Whilst musical performers may often feel that their livelihoods depend on the approval of the conductor, they would usually have more than one performance in which to prove themselves. In this respect, an inspection is more like a trial. It is dominated by the verdict. The oscillation of emotion and opinion which can occur in a trial also happens in an inspection; people move back and forth from optimism to pessimism.

People hold similar positivist expectations of the legal profession as they do of inspection. Legal judgement does have a stronger burden of proof than inspection, but the verdict ultimately depends on the corporate findings of the jury. However, although we might hope that teachers would have a similar confidence to someone who stands in the dock knowing they are innocent, this would be to lose inspection's developmental dimension. Justice must be seen to be done, but in an inspection the justice is being applied to a process – of defining professionalism. In the courtroom, we understand the difference between innocence and guilt; in inspection the core concepts are being generated while they are used.

de Bono (1990) draws attention to the 'rock-logic', which he sees as pervading much of Western, logical, thought, and advocates a move towards 'water-logic' by which the rigidities of oppositional thinking flow forward together. This thinking is only a different image of the synthesis that follows thesis and antithesis but it does help to illustrate the fluidity of inspection. In the analysis of the case studies, there have been several elements which have come in pairs: judgement or development; technical or emotional; ownership or displacement; ritual or real; positivist or humanist; impartial or value-laden. These elements could be built into a construct to represent inspection: a tableau of bodies, mutually dependent, at a circus; or a cantilever bridge which needs one half to keep the other in balance. But these constructs are too rigid to be truly representative. The balances are transitory and the elements are in motion – more like a whirlpool with a stick poised at its edge before being sucked in. But the misrepresentation would remain if inspection were seen as all fluid. Inspection is constructed around an essential hierarchy: the inspector inspects the inspected.

Conclusion

My original notion of inspection was rather simplistic. I had seen it as a singular event in the life of a school – a visit by a team of inspectors to an institution. The case studies have shown it to be much more complex: a collection of interactions between and among inspectors, the headteacher, teachers and governors. The subtleties of judgement, perception and learning make an assessment of the effects of inspection difficult.

My central research question asked: how does a full inspection affect the life of a primary school and, in particular, the quality of its management of learning?

There can be little doubt that the inspections I have studied have left a significant mark on the professional lives of their participants. It has been less clear how long these effects might last, or whether there will be other consequences, developmental or otherwise, on the quality of the teaching and learning in the schools. Several headteachers and teachers have suggested that their inspections will have a positive effect, although there have been others who have been dismissive of potential benefit. To track the effects of inspection as they percolate through a school and its staff's professional consciousness would need further research.

I asked at the outset whether the effects of inspection could be measured. It is possible that the tightening of action planning under the new Ofsted procedures will make it easier to demonstrate that inspections do contribute to a school's improvement. However, the measurement of development will remain problematic. There are too many variables and too many qualitative factors.

Whilst I have tried to resist an evaluative stance, it is important to consider not only whether inspection has benefits, but also whether its benefits outweigh its costs. These costs have not only been monetary; there has been considerable human cost. In so far as my research might itself make a difference, it has demonstrated both the significance of professional confidence to the success of inspection and the significance of inspection to professional confidence. The making sense of things, so much a part of this project and of these case studies, is central to the learning process. So also is self-esteem.

APPENDIX:

THE CASE STUDIES

Case study 1

A suburban junior school of nine classes. The inspection was mounted by the LEA because adverse publicity in the press had called the management of the school into question. In the event, the inspectors validated the school's management and apparently helped to dispel some of the high emotions which had been running in the school's community. The inspection was carried out by four inspectors.

Research data: interviews with the headteacher, three teachers, the school secretary and one inspector.

Case study 2

A village first school with four classes. This inspection was the LEA's response to HMI concern over correspondence from the headteacher to senior political figures about Key Stage 1 Standard Assessment Tasks. The inspectors seem to have decided very quickly that the school was meeting its obligations under the National Curriculum and subsequently moved to a developmental agenda. A report jointly written by teachers and inspectors was proposed but was never actually completed. The inspection was carried out by three inspectors.

Research data: interviews with the headteacher, four teachers, the school secretary and one inspector.

Case study 3

A suburban middle school with 16 classes. In this inspection, a group of LEA inspectors who all shared responsibilities for arts subjects negotiated with the school to inspect its arts provision. The headteacher had originally welcomed this opportunity, despite the fact that the arts were not a priority in the school's development plan. In the event, there was some resentment that the inspectors did not validate the school's arts provision in the way that had been anticipated; there was a suggestion that the inspection had been an unhelpful distraction. The inspectors wrote separate reports on their subjects; the lead inspector wrote a digest of the overall findings. The inspection was carried out by five inspectors.

Research data: interviews with the headteacher, four teachers and five inspectors; a log of the inspection – before, during and afterwards – by one of the teachers interviewed.

Case study 4

An urban junior school with eight classes. This LEA had established a cycle for reviewing schools, with a full inspection every four years. The inspection was carried out according to a published set of procedures. A report was written and shared with the governors. A feature of this inspection was the fact that it was led by the school's local inspector, a practice usually avoided by the LEA. Both the inspectors and the school viewed the inspection very positively, although there were casualties and suggestions that the report had avoided some issues which might have been less palatable for the school. The inspection was carried out by five inspectors.

Research data: interviews with the headteacher, four teachers, two governors and four inspectors.

Case study 5

An urban primary school with 11 classes. This was an HMI inspection conducted according to the Ofsted framework but also as part of its survey of schools in deprived urban areas. I participated in the inspection as a trainee Ofsted inspector. It had a fully published report. The inspection was carried out by five HMI and two Ofsted trainees.

Research data: my log of the inspection.

Case study 6

A suburban first school with eight classes. This, like case study 4, was an LEA inspection undertaken as part of a review cycle. The LEA had determined that a sample of schools due for an external review would be reported as a full inspection to the education committee. One member of the team was the school's local support inspector. The school had seen the inspection as validating its development and overall provision. This case study revealed that the impact of an inspection can die away quite quickly. The research interviews were conducted eight months after the inspection and there were few traces of any lasting effects. The inspection was carried out by three LEA inspectors after the passing of the 1992 Education (Schools) Act, but before the publication of the Ofsted framework for Inspection.

Research data: interviews with the headteacher, three teachers and two inspectors.

Case study 7

A village primary school with four classes. Again, this inspection was part of an LEA review cycle. However, its report did not go before the education committee. The headteacher was the only person who received a full copy of the report. He had presented only extracts to the governors and to the staff. This inspection was complicated by the resistance of the headteacher to inspection which had led to his being rather elusive about making the necessary arrangements. The inspectors seem to have based their work on the framework for inspection but the school did not seem aware of the criteria used. Because this was a very small school, it was not possible for any report to hide the identity of the teachers concerned. The inspection was carried out by three inspectors.

Research data: interviews with the headteacher, two teachers, the school secretary and one inspector.

Case study 8

An inner-urban first school with ten classes. This school was one of a sample of LEA schools inspected each year. It was identified through its earlier participation in a curriculum development project. The LEA had a set of procedures by which it reviewed a number of schools each year in order to report on the health of its schools to the education committee. Although these procedures were used, they were somewhat distorted by the additional use of the Ofsted framework. This case distinguished itself as the most negative of all the cases I researched. The findings were negative, relationships between the inspectors and the staff were often strained, the inspection team itself experienced considerable internal tensions, and there were several procedural inconsistencies. There was a written report of the inspection which was delivered after an unusually long delay. The inspection was carried out by five inspectors.

Research data: interviews with the headteacher, three teachers, two governors and two inspectors.

Case study 9

A suburban junior school with eight classes. The LEA team was following a well-established procedure for reviewing schools on a four-yearly cycle. The local support inspector was deliberately excluded from the team to add to its objectivity. Two members of the team had recently been trained for Ofsted inspections. As a result, the style of the inspection was sometimes more direct than the school had anticipated. The report was internal to the school. This case was distinctive in the way that the inspectors struggled to balance a generally positive set of findings with their concern over two particular teachers. The inspection was carried out by four inspectors.

Research data: interviews with the headteacher, three teachers and two inspectors.

Case study 10

A suburban junior school with ten classes. This was a pilot Ofsted inspection carried out by an LEA team using the Ofsted framework. I was the lead inspector and I was also the school's support inspector. The school had put itself forward for one of these pilot inspections but had not expected the formality of its style nor the criticisms of its report. The report was shared with the governors but not with the parents. The inspection was carried out by five inspectors.

Research data: interviews with the headteacher, and three teachers carried out by a third party using a prepared schedule; interviews with two inspectors carried out by researcher; researcher's log of the inspection.

Case study 11

A suburban junior school with 12 classes. This was also a pilot Ofsted inspection carried out by an LEA team using the Ofsted framework. The school had also put itself forward for one of these inspections. In this case, the headteacher knew that there were difficult issues to be addressed. Nevertheless, the school did not appear to have anticipated the extent to which the inspectors would uncover deficiencies. The report was shared with the governors but not with the parents. The inspection was carried out by five inspectors.

Research data: interviews with the headteacher, four teachers and three inspectors.

Case study 12

An urban primary school with 13 classes. This was an HMI inspection conducted under Ofsted procedures and used as an opportunity to train two
potential registered Ofsted inspectors. The lead inspector for this inspection
was changed at the last minute. As a result the staff were briefed twice with
significant contrasts in the style of the two lead inspectors. The inspection
also departed from standard HMI/Ofsted procedures in that a feedback staff
meeting was held. The report was published externally as well as internally
to the school. The inspection was carried out by a team of seven inspectors,
of whom two were Ofsted trainees.

Research data: interviews with the headteacher, three teachers and two
inspectors.

BIBLIOGRAPHY

Alexander, R. (1991) *Primary Education in Leeds*. Leeds: University of Leeds.

Alexander, R. (1992) *Policy and Practice in Primary Education*. London: Routledge and Kegan Paul.

Audit Commission (1989) *Assuring Quality in Education*. London: HMSO.

Auld, R. (1976) *William Tyndale Junior and Infants Schools Public Enquiry*. London: Inner London Education Authority.

Becher, A. (1978) Ends, means and policies, in A. Becher and S. Maclure (eds) *Accountability in Education*. Slough: NFER Nelson.

Becher, A. and Eraut, M. (1982) Accountability in the middle years of schooling, in R. McCormick (ed.) *Calling Education to Account*. London: Heinemann/The Open University.

Becher, A., Eraut, M. and Knight, J. (1981) *Policies for Educational Accountability*. London: Heinemann.

Becker, H. (1982) Problems of inference and proof, in R. McCormick (ed.) *Calling Education to Account*. London: Heinemann/The Open University.

Beeby, C. (1977) The meaning of evaluation, *Current Issues in Education*, 4(1): 68–78.

Bernstein, B., Elvin, H. and Peters, R. (1966) Ritual in education, *Philosophical Transactions of the Royal Society of London*, Series B, 164(251): 429–36.

Biott, C. and Nias, J. (eds) (1992) *Working and Learning Together for Change*. Buckingham: Open University Press.

Bolam, R., Smith, G. and Canter, H. (1978) *LEA Advisers and the Mechanisms of Innovation*. Slough: NFER Nelson.

Bruner, J. (1967) *Towards a Theory of Instruction*. Cambridge, Mass.: Harvard University Press.

Burgess, R. (1985) *Strategies in Educational Research*. Lewes: Falmer.

Burgess, R. (ed.) (1985) *Issues in Educational Research, Qualitative Methods*. Lewes: Falmer.

Coleman, P. and Larocque, L. (1990) *Struggling to be Good Enough*. Lewes: Falmer.

Dean, J. (1982) Evaluation and advisers, in R. McCormick (ed.) *Calling Education to Account*. London: Heinemann/The Open University.

de Bono, E. (1990) *I am Right; You are Wrong*. London: Viking.

Delves, A. and Watts, J. (1979) A year of evaluation, in R. McCormick (ed.) *Calling Education to Account*. London: Heinemann/The Open University.

Department of Education and Science (1983) *The Work of HM Inspectorate in England and Wales (the Raynor Report)*. London: HMSO.

Department of Education and Science (1985) *Draft Statement on the Role of Local Education Authority Advisory Services*. London: HMSO.

Department of Education and Science (1985) *HM Inspectors Today: Standards in Education*. London: HMSO.

Durkheim, E. (1938) *The Rules of Sociological Method*. London: Collier-MacMillan.

Easen, P. (1991) The visible supporter with no invisible means of support, in C. Biott (ed.) *Semi-detached Teachers*. London: Falmer.

Eraut, M. (1978) Accountability at school level, some options and their implications, in A. Becher and S. Maclure (eds) *Accountability in Education*. Slough: NFER Nelson.

Eraut, M. (1992) *Developing the Professions: Training, Quality and Accountability – University of Sussex Professorial Lecture*. Brighton: University of Sussex.

Friedson, E. (ed.) (1973) *The Professions and their Prospects*. London: Sage.

Goodlad, S. (1984) *Education for the Professions*. Guildford: NFER Nelson.

Goodwin, F. (1968) *The Art of the Headmaster*. London: Ward Lock Educational.

Gray, H. (ed.) (1988) *Management Consultancy in Schools*. London: Cassell.

Handy, C. (1976) *Understanding Organisations*. Harmondsworth: Penguin.

Hargreaves, A. (1985) The micro–macro problem in the sociology of education, in R.G. Burgess (ed.) *Issues in Educational Research, Qualitative Methods*. Lewes: Falmer.

Harland, J. (1990) *The Work and Impact of Advisory Teachers*. Slough: NFER.

Harris, T. (1973) *I'm OK, You're OK*. London: Pan.

Heller, H. (1988) The advisory service and consultancy, in H. Gray (ed.) *Management Consultancy in Schools*. London: Cassell.

Henkel, M. (1991) *Government, Evaluation and Change*. London: Jessica Kingsley.

Her Majesty's Inspectorate (1985–9) *Curriculum Matters* (series). London: HMSO.

Her Majesty's Inspectorate (1988–91) *Aspects of Primary Education* (series). London: HMSO.

House of Commons Select Committee on Education (1986) *Achievement in Primary Schools*. London: HMSO.

Inner London Education Authority (1977) *Keeping the School Under Review*. London: Inner London Education Authority.

Inner London Education Authority (1988) *Primary Language Record*. London: Inner London Education Authority.

Lawton, D. (1988) The contemporary role of HMI in England, *Journal of Educational Policy*, 3(2): 191–6.

Lawton, D. and Gordon, P. (1987) *HMI*. London: Routledge and Kegan Paul.

McCormick, R. (ed.) (1982) *Calling Education to Account*. London: Heinemann/The Open University.

McCormick, R. and James, M. (1983) *Curriculum Evaluation in Schools*. London: Croom Helm.

MacDonald, B. (1978) Accountability, standards and the process of schooling, in A. Becher and S. Maclure (eds) *Accountability in Education*. Slough: NFER Nelson.

Marjoram, T. (1989) *Assessing Schools*. London: Kogan Page.

Maychell, K. and Keys, W. (1993) *Under Inspection*. Slough: NFER.

Mezirow, J. (1992) A practical theory of adult learning and education, in C. Biott and

J. Nias (eds) *Working and Learning Together for Change*. Buckingham: Open University Press.

Millett, A. (1992) Speech to Hampshire headteachers and governors, Lyndhurst, Hampshire, 30 November 1993.

Moore, T. (1992) *Care of the Soul*. New York: Harper-Collins.

National Association of Educational Inspectors, Advisers and Consultants (1993) *Briefing No. 2*. Haywards Heath: NAEIAC.

Office for Standards in Education (1992) *Framework for the Inspection of Schools*. London: HMSO.

Parlett, M. and Dearden, G. (1977) *Introduction to Illuminative Evaluation*. Cardiff-by-the-Sea: Pacific Soundings Press.

Pearce, J. (1986) *Standards and the LEA – the Accountability of Schools*. Slough: NFER Nelson.

Peters, R. (1966) *Ethics and Education*. London: Allen and Unwin.

Piaget, J. (1950) *The Psychology of Intelligence*. London: Routledge and Kegan Paul.

Roberts, C. (1985) *The Interview Game*. London: BBC.

Schön, D. (1987) *Educating the Reflective Practitioner*. London: Jossey-Bass.

Shipman, M. (ed.) (1985) *Educational Research, Principles, Policies and Practices*. Lewes: Falmer.

Simons, H. (1982) Conversation piece – the practice of interviewing in case study research, in R. McCormick (ed.) *Calling Education to Account*. London: Heinemann/The Open University.

Sockett, H. (ed.) (1980) *Accountability and the English Educational System*. Sevenoaks: Hodder and Stoughton.

Sockett, H. (1982) Accountability, purpose and meaning, in R. McCormick (ed.) *Calling Education to Account*. London: Heinemann/The Open University.

Stillman, A. and Grant, M. (1989) *The LEA Adviser – a Changing Role*. Slough: NFER Nelson.

Wilcox, B. (1992) *Time-Constrained Evaluation*. London: Routledge.

Winkley, D. (1985) *Diplomats and Detectives – LEA Advisers at Work*. London: Robert Royce.

Wright-Mills, C. (1959) *The Sociological Imagination*. New York: Oxford University Press.

INDEX

ROLES AND RESPONSIBILITIES IN THE PRIMARY SCHOOL
CHANGING DEMANDS, CHANGING PRACTICES

Rosemary Webb and Graham Vulliamy

- How are teachers planning and implementing the National Curriculum at Key Stage 2?

- How have the recent policy and legislative changes affected the roles and responsibilities of class teachers, currriculum coordinators, deputy headteachers and headteachers?

- How are primary schools managing the current plethora of innovations and what can be learned from their experience?

Based on qualitative research in 50 schools throughout England and Wales, this book portrays teachers' work as it is currently experienced in the post-ERA context of multiple innovations. It examines the impact of the National Curriculum and assessment on classroom practice, curriculum organization and planning at Key Stage 2. Drawing on the wealth of ideas and successful practices shared with the authors by the teachers in the study, it demonstrates how class teachers, curriculum coordinators, deputy headteachers and headteachers are tackling the new demands of their expanding roles. An analysis of the management of change reveals a growing tension between collegial and top-down directive managerial styles, which is fundamentally affecting the culture of primary schools. Through presenting what is actually happening in primary schools in contrast to prescribed educational orthodoxies, this book makes a vital contribution to the debate on the future of primary education.

Contents

Introduction and methodology – The changing context of primary education – Changing demands on classroom practice – Changing curriculum organization and planning – The changing role of the curriculum coordinator – The changing role of the deputy headteacher – The changing role of the headteacher – Managing whole school change in the post-ERA primary school – References – Index.

192pp   0 335 19472 9 (Paperback)   0 335 19473 7 (Hardback)

TEACHABLE MOMENTS
THE ART OF TEACHING IN PRIMARY SCHOOLS
Peter Woods and Bob Jeffrey

Creative teaching is an art form – aesthetic, intuitive and expressive. The recent proliferation of new educational policies and the related increase in tensions and dilemmas facing schools, combined with the growing demand for a wider range of skills and knowledge among children mean that there is an even greater need for creative teaching than before the National Curriculum.

This book addresses this need by:
• exploring the features of creative teaching with a focus on the day to day practice of primary teachers;
• showing how teachers use emotion, create atmosphere and stimulate imagination to enhance their teaching;
• examining the ways in which teachers have managed the National Curriculum and developed a new professional discourse in response to government pressures.

This book is a sequel to *Creative Teachers in Primary Schools* (Open University Press, 1995) and builds upon this work to provide new insights into the art of teaching.

Contents
Preface – Creative teaching and its significance – Creative teachers – A new professional discourse? Adjusting to managerialism – The emotional side of teaching and learning – Creating atmosphere and tone – Stimulating the imagination through story – Managing the curriculum – References – Index.

176pp   0 335 19373 0 (Paperback)   0 335 19374 9 (Hardback)

EDUCATING THE WHOLE CHILD
CROSS-CURRICULAR SKILLS, THEMES AND DIMENSIONS
John and Iram Siraj-Blatchford (eds)

This book approaches the 'delivery' of the cross-curricular skills, themes and dimensions from a perspective emphasizing the culture of primary schools and the social worlds of children. The authors argue that the teaching of skills, attitudes, concepts and knowledge to young children should not be seen as separate or alternative objectives, but rather as complementary and essential elements of the educational process. It is the teacher's role to help children develop and build upon the understandings, skills, knowledge and attitudes which they bring with them into school. Learning for young children is a social activity where new skills and understandings are gained through interaction with both adults and with their peers. Each of the approaches outlined in the book is thus grounded in an essential respect and empathy for children and childhood as a distinct stage in life and not merely a preparation for the world of adulthood. For instance, the authors argue that responsibilities and decision-making are everyday experiences for children and that they need to be able to develop attitudes and skills which enable them to participate fully in their own social world.

Contents

Cross-curricular skills, themes and dimensions: an introduction – Little citizens: helping children to help each other – Effective schooling for all: the 'special educational needs' dimension – Racial equality education: identity, curriculum and pedagogy – 'Girls don't do bricks': gender and sexuality in the primary classroom – Children in an economic world: young children learning in a consumerist and post-industrial society – Catching them young: careers education in the primary years – Understanding environmental education for the primary classroom – Health education in the primary school: back to basics? – The place of PSE in the primary school – Index.

Contributors

John Bennett, Debra Costley, Debbie Epstein, Peter Lang, Val Millman, Lina Patel, Alistair Ross, Ann Sinclair Taylor, Iram Siraj-Blatchford, John Siraj-Blatchford, Balbir Kaur Sohal, Janice Wale.

192pp   0 335 19444 3 (paperback)   0 335 19445 1 (hardback)